ON EDUCATION

ON EDUCATION

Jane Addams

With a new introduction by
Ellen Condliffe Lagemann

Transaction Publishers
New Brunswick (U.S.A.) and London (U.K.)

Fifth printing 2009

New material this edition copyright © 1994 by Transaction Publishers, New Brunswick, New Jersey. Originally published in 1985 by Teachers College Press.

Library of Congress Catalog Number: 93-47022
ISBN: 978-1-56000-734-0
Printed in the United States of America

Library of Congress Cataloging-in-Publication Data

Addams, Jane, 1869-1935.
    On education / Jane Addams ; edited and with a new introduction by Ellen Condliffe Lagemann.
        p. cm
    Originally published: Jane Addams on education. New York : Teachers College Press, 1985.
    Includes bibliographical references.
    ISBN: 1-56000-734-6
        1. Education—Philosophy. 2. Progressive education—United States—Philosophy—History. 3. Social reformers—United States—Biography. 4. Social service—United States—History. I. Lagemann, Ellen Condliffe, 1945- II. Title.

LB875.A33A3 1994   93-47022
370'.1—dc20   CIP

CONTENTS

Introduction to the Transaction Edition   vii

Introduction to the Original Edition   1

Bibliographic Essay   43

Selections

1. The Subjective Necessity for
   Social Settlements (*1893*)   49
2. The College Woman and
   the Family Claim (*1898*)   64
3. A Function of the Social Settlement (*1899*)   74
4. Educational Methods (*1902*)   98
5. The Humanizing Tendency of
   Industrial Education (*1904*)   120
6. Child Labor Legislation — A Requisite for
   Industrial Efficiency (*1905*)   124
7. The Public School and the
   Immigrant Child (*1908*)   136
8. The House of Dreams (*1909*)   143
9. Immigrants and Their Children (*1910*)   162
10. Socialized Education (*1910*)   172
11. Recreation as a Public Function
    in Urban Communities (*1911*)   186

12. Moral Education and Legal Protection
    for Children (*1912*)   192
13. Widening the Circle of Enlightenment:
    Hull House and Adult Education (*1930*)   204
14. Education by the Current Event (*1930*)   212

Acknowledgments   225

INTRODUCTION TO THE TRANSACTION EDITION
Why Read Jane Addams?

In contemplating why it makes sense to republish *On Education,* it occured to me that important thinkers leave writings that engage people differently at different times. One can read Jane Addams to learn about social problems at the turn of the century, about social settlements and sociology, about women's lives, or, as in this collection, about education broadly conceived. Reading Addams can be instructive in a number of different ways.

When I first read Addams as a college student, I was especially interested in her life at Hull House, the settlement she and Ellen Gates Starr founded in Chicago in 1889. Although other settlements sprang up in cities across the United States—there were some four hundred settlements in the United States by 1910—Hull House was widely acknowledged as "the settlement of settlements" and Jane Addams was "its moving power."[1]

A person of powerful intellect and deep-seated ideals, Addams also possessed an unusual capacity for empathy and compassion. The combination caused her as a young adult to seek out a life that would allow her to put her education to work for other people. She was not a selfless "saint" ready to sacrifice herself for the unfortunate. Rather she was a person who seems early to have realized that existing roles, especially those available to well-educated, middle-class, Victorian-American women, did not suit her and that realization stoked the purposiveness and drive she needed to sustain a long search for an alternative, which she finally began to recognize and develop after visiting Toynbee Hall, a settlement established by Oxford graduates in the East End of London in 1884.[2] Addams's life was, of course, extraordinary, "notable," and unusual, and yet, it was also filled with experiences that are relatively common among young people, especially young women. Because her writings reveal a good deal about her life, they can illuminate and legitimate many of the aspirations, frustrations, strains, and anxieties that are enduring elements in the transition to adulthood for many youth.

On a less personal level, Addams's writings are worth reading as powerful statements of a profoundly humane, deeply democratic philosophy. More than any contemporary writer of whom I am aware (with the possible exception of William James), she built her philosophy from her own experiences filtered through images and ideas acquired through reading, study, travel, and self-reflection. Addams's writing style tended to be autobiographical in focus and informal in tone, and this had contradictory consequences. On the one hand, it made her writing easy to mistake for "mere autobiography," nothing more than stories from one person's life; on the other hand, it transformed generalizations into unusually incisive experiential interpretations of social situations and problems. Although Addams never presented her views as a formal "philosophy," that is what her deeper observations about social and political relationships actually were with the narrative record of people and events serving as a foil.

Within Addams's philosophy, three convictions were central. The first had to do with the importance of "community" for life in a democratic society. Addams thought that industrialism and patterns of population settlement in the nation's growing cities had diminished possibilities for community by forcing unfortunate divisions between different groups of people, especially between employers and employees and the established and the newly arrived. In consequence, purposeful efforts needed to be mounted to rebuild the conditions that had once made the behaviors and spirit of neighborliness spontaneous aspects of community life.[3]

Closely related was the belief that settlement work should simultaneously fulfill "objective" and "subjective" necessities. Efforts merely to relieve the poverty, disease, malnutrition, and alienation—the "objective" needs—so evident right outside Hull House's front door would have less long-term benefit, Addams thought, than efforts that combined assistance to the needy with opportunities for effective altruism among privileged youth in search of ways to enact their ideals.[4] Obviously drawing on her own experience, Addams believed that the young women who ran a clinic to help mothers learn about nutrition or the University of Chicago professors who talked with groups of workers eager to learn about the history of the labor movement gained as much from the services they provided as did the settlement's neighbors. Moralistic and controlling forms of charity were frowned upon; reciprocity was acknowledged and highly valued.

Last but hardly least important, Jane Addams's philosophy was premised on the belief that social progress required a synthesis of study and action, science and social reform. Addams is reported to have said that "the work of the settlement" was to translate knowledge into terms of life.[5] Her commitment to the integration of social investigation and social improvement made Hull House something of an open university where a constant flow of talk about politics, ideas, public events, art, philosophy, and the immediate problems of a destitute family or a gang of neighborhood boys provided constantly evolving and lived meaning to such abstract concepts as citizenship, culture, assimilation, and education.

Addams once characterized Hull House as:

> an experimental effort to aid in the solution of the social and industrial problems which are engendered by the modern conditions of life in a great city. It insists that these problems are not confined to any one portion of a city. It is an attempt to relieve, at the same time, the overaccumulation at one end of society and the destitution at the other.... From its very nature it can stand for no political or social propaganda.... The one thing to be dreaded in the Settlement is that it lose its flexibility, its power of quick adaptation, its readiness to change its methods as its environment may demand. It must be open to conviction and must have a deep and abiding sense of tolerance. It must be hospitable and ready for experiment. It should demand from its residents a scientific patience in the accumulation of facts.... It must be grounded in a philosophy whose foundation is on the solidarity of the human race... Its residents must be emptied of all conceit of opinion and all self-assertion.... They must be content to live quietly side by side with

their neighbors, until they grow into a sense of relationship and mutual interests. . . . They are bound to see the
needs of their neighbors as a whole, to furnish data or
legislation, and to use their influence to secure it. In short,
residents are pledged to devote themselves to the duties
of good citizenship and to the arousing of the social energies which too largely lie dormant in every neighborhood given over to industrialism. They are bound to
regard the entire life of their city as organic, to make an
effort to unify and to protest against its over-
diffrentiation.[6]

According to her own description of it, Hull House
was an institution dedicated to social improvement, and
open to change, novelty, and experimentation. It was
an institution "grounded in philosophy" as an approach
to life, a means for examining one's actions in light of
the new problems and situations those actions revealed.
The philosophy Addams developed, tested, and refined
at Hull House humanized political and social problems
not merely by demanding that something concrete be
done to address them, but more profoundly by interpreting them in terms of real-life people and situations.
It demonstrated the intellectual power and reform energy that can be mustered when philosophy is understood as constantly evolving insight derived from
systematic, open thinking about the problems of the
world.

A social thinker of first rank, who directed her intelligence toward immediate, practical issues rather than
the elaboration of knowledge for its own sake, Addams
managed to avoid many of the epistemological constraints that grew up early in the twentieth century as
research universities came to exercise more and more

importance in the processes through which knowledge is defined. Within these universities, research and teaching was divided into ever more specialized and isolated departments and divisions and different bodies of knowledge came to be linked to particular professions. Having once encompassed philosophy, psychology, and the social sciences, a synthetic subject like moral philosophy was now divided into many smaller fields; and these smaller fields were articulated with different professions, philosophy being joined to the theological professions, psychology to health and education, and the various social sciences to social work and business. This yielded tremendous gains in the elaboration and refinement of the different sciences, but it did not always result in more effective ways to understand and address complex social problems, which often fell outside the scope of a single discipline or profession. Having never pursued advanced graduate study and having never sought or held a university position, Addams remained outside the disciplinary and professional structures that came increasingly to organize what scholars taught and studied and even how they thought. As I argued at greater length in the original introduction to *On Education,* this, combined with gender-related stereotyping, resulted in a discount on Addams's stature as an intellectual. Although she was an astute sociologist, her writings lacked the cachet of university "science" and, if read today, they are more likely read as historic documents than as statements of social philosophy or enduringly valuable commentaries on social dynamics.

That Addams has not received her due as a thinker is unfortunate, and it is especially unfortunate because her remove from developments in the academy enabled her to develop and sustain an approach to social analysis that was broad, synthetic, and problem– as opposed to discipline– or profession-centered. Although this is old-fashioned in the sense that it resembles social science of the "pre-professional," nineteenth-century variety, Addams's broad, synthetic, problem-centered approach can encourage fundamental rethinking of seemingly settled issues. This may be especially important in studying education. Indeed, it is because Addams's writings on education invite fundamental reconsideration of the way we organize and think about education that they are worth reading still.

Although some normal schools and teacher's institutes were established during the nineteenth century, education did not become a field of formal study until the very end of the century. Its development was spurred by a growing demand for teacher training, which encouraged the newly established research universities to establish schools of education. As this occured and a "science of education" began to be developed, the scope of thinking about education was narrowed to suit the curricular needs of teachers in training. This resulted in a tendancy to focus on children to the exclusion of adults, on schools to the exclusion of families, universities, and cultural institutions, and on techniques of instruction, guidance, and administration to the exclusion of analysis of educational purposes, possibilities, and problems. The consequences of this narrow conception of "educational science" were unfortunate for teachers, who generally did not receive an education that could equip them to go beyond transmitting knowledge to transforming it in ways that would render it relevant and accessible to the experience of all students. What is more, the narrow, technical conception of "educational science" that emerged in the research universities established an equally narrow template for public thinking about education. In consequence, education, a process of growth, came commonly to be confused with schooling, the institution most directly organized to promote that process, and the reformist potential of education writ large was generally lost from sight. Consideration of how, say, the media of communication (for better and worse) shape people's thinking and behavior was now ruled out of education, which was seen increasingly in terms of preparation for life, especially preparation for work.

Of course, it is not at all certain that education writ large could have provided the social compass some turn-of-the-century thinkers, including Addams's close friend and colleague, John Dewey, were searching for.[7] The point, though, is that possibilities for promoting greater equality and wider participation in culture and politics through education were not fully tested because the power of education was narrowed to fit the institutional constraints of schools. Lost for a time, those possibilities still exist, however, and deserve to be explored and considered in a variety of contexts.

Jane Addams's writings can be helpful in this regard. They enable one to step back in time to ponder anew, apart from existing school-centered assumptions about educational research, practice, and policy, what education can offer a large, complex, advanced industrial democracy. Because Jane Addams remained aloof from most "professional" thinking about education she understood that an infinite variety of experiences, associated with an infinite variety of institutions and sometimes not associated with any institution, can shape, extend, elaborate, refine, and otherwise change the ways in which people perceive themselves and their surroundings, are able to act in relation to those perceptions, and can associate for purposes of thought and action with other people. She was also able to recognize that some aspects of education, like some aspects of life experience more generally, could not be planned, anticipated, or explained. In addition, her own experience taught her that too exclusive a focus on formal instruction and study—or, as she put it, too much time devoted to "lumbering our minds with literature"— could have miseducative consequences.[8] All these insights and many more are evident in Addams writings on education and they offer important grist for rethinking what education can and cannot do.

Why read Jane Addams, then? There are many reasons, but one overall. Addams was an astute observer of human society and a smart analyst of human motivations and behaviors. Because her writings were grounded in her own experience, they convey a sense of the embeddedness of psychological, philosophical, or educational problems in the complexities of daily life. Having not given in to the modern penchant for categorizing experiences and separating them into distinct compartments Addams's thought cannot be neatly pigeon-holed and set aside. Often startling and evocative, it forces one to think. Surely that is sufficient reason for this new edition of *On Education.*

Ellen Condliffe Lagemann

NOTES

1. For a general history that includes estimates of numbers see Allen Davis, *Spearheads for Reform: The Social Settlements and the Progressive Movement, 1890–1914* (1967; New Brunswick: Rutgers University Press, 1984), p.12. The two quotes are from Nicholas Kelley, "Early Days at Hull House." *Social Service Review* 28 (December 1934), 424; and Alice Hamilton to Grace Abbott, May 20, 1935, in Barbara Sicherman, *Alice Hamilton: A Life in Letters* (Cambridge: Harvard Univesity Press, 1984), p.354.
2. For a recent discussion of Toynbee Hall see Mina Carson, *Settlement Folk: Social Thought and the American Settlement Movement, 1885–1930* (Chicago: University of Chicago Press, 1990),pp. 31–34.
3. Riva Shpak Lissak, *Pluralism and Progressives: Hull House and the New Immigrants, 1890–1919* (Chicago: University of Chicago Press, 1989) claims that such efforts were actually a failure, Hull House having had little effect on its immigrant neighbors.
4. Robyn Muncy, *Creating A Female Dominion in American Reform, 1890–1935* (New York: Oxford University Press, 1991), chap.1, argues that Hull House had a more particular, feminist purpose, having been purposefully designed to provide an institutionalized setting in which women could directly exercise power.
5. Alice Hamilton to Agnes Hamilton, June 23rd [18]99, in Sicherman, *Alice Hamilton,* p. 133.
6. Jane Addams, *Twenty Years at Hull-House* (New York: Macmillian, 1910), p. 125–127.
7. Dewey's high faith in education as the central means of social progress emerged during his years at the University of Chicago (1894–1904), when he was actively involved at Hull House. It is expressed most clearly in the first lecture of *School and Society* [1899] in John Dewey, *The Middle Works 1899-1924,* ed. Jo Ann Boydston (Carbondale: University of Southern Illinois Press,1976): I: 5–20. For a discussion of Dewey's chang-

ing views over time see Robert B. Westbrook, *John Dewey and American Democracy* (Ithaca: Cornell University Press, 1991).
8. Addams, *Twenty Years at Hull House.*, p.66.

INTRODUCTION
Jane Addams:
An Educational
Biography

In September of 1889, Jane Addams moved to an immigrant slum neighborhood on the West Side of Chicago. With Ellen Gates Starr, a close college friend, she had rented the top floor of the former Charles J. Hull mansion in order to live and work with the poor. The social settlement that was established in this way, which was called Hull House, quickly became a vital neighborhood center as well as a meeting place for men and women from all walks of life and from all over the world. It provided a variety of services to the people of its neighborhood, among them a day nursery, a savings bank, a medical dispensary, and a kitchen that sold hot meals to workers in nearby factories. It sponsored innumerable clubs for children and college extension courses for office and factory workers. It helped to organize a Working People's Chorus and a Paderewski Club (for the musically inclined), a Nineteenth Ward Improvement Club, and a Working People's Social Science Club, where nonneighborhood scholars, journalists, ministers, and politicians could meet and debate with neighborhood people. As it became known that Hull House was "on the side of the Unions," the settlement also became a center for trade-union organization, a headquarters for striking workers, and a place where strikers and employers could talk and find help in mediating their differences.[1]

To support Hull House and to explain its program and philosophy to the general public, Jane Addams devoted a great deal of time to public speaking and writing. At the settlement, in collaboration with increasing numbers of other residents, she tried to understand and find ways to alleviate the immediate daily problems of the people of the Hull House neighborhood. Then, in her public statements, she set forth what had been learned at Hull House and how this pertained to larger, more general, and often better known social problems and principles. The result was not only an institution that was suffused with a truly humane spirit of inquiry, but also a corpus of writings in which many aspects of turn-of-the-century American society were wisely and constructively criticized, and the nature and social implications of democracy, incisively explored.

Central to the view of democracy that Addams developed during the forty-four years she lived at Hull House was a vision of a society in which all individuals, regardless of gender, ethnicity, race, or economic status, would have the opportunity fully to express and to develop their talents, interests, and ambitions. Addams believed that democracy required true reciprocity and free accommodation between different individuals and groups, and she was convinced that this could only be achieved in a society where social goods like freedom could be guaranteed to the individual because they were guaranteed to all. Addams's view of democracy was, of course, based on a view of human nature. She recognized the existence of self-interest and potential conflicts of interest, but she also held the optimistic belief that all human beings were adaptable and capable of responding to new experiences and environmental change. Not surprisingly, therefore, her view of democracy was built on the insistent conviction that all people could be led to see that they had a self-interest — a self-interest that was also a common social interest — in the protection and fulfillment of the interests of others. Education was the basis for democracy as Jane Addams understood it, and her writings offer insights into education that remain profound.

Addams viewed education broadly. She believed that it included more than purposeful teaching and learning within a formally organized instructional setting. Hence, in her writings she tended to approach education by considering the consequences, in terms of behavior, social sensibilities, and attitudes toward self and others, of existing and possible patterns of social relationship and of available and needed opportunities for meaningful work, recreation, growth, and renewal. She focused on whether and how social relationships (domestic, familial, occupational, political, intergenerational, and intergroup) allowed and promoted free expression for all parties. She queried the degree to which such relationships offered chances to develop a fuller understanding of how one's job, social status, or immediate personal dilemma was related to the historical traditions and social systems of which it was a part. And she raised questions about whether and how such relationships supported and fostered the self-esteem, awareness, energy, and curiosity that were necessary to well-being and continuing growth.

In her writings, Addams also described the variety

of impulses manifested by people of different ages—
the impulse to imagine and play so evident in young
children, the impulse to make idealistic commitments
so prevalent among young adults, and the impulse to
nurture and teach so important for mature men and
women. And she explored the ways in which these impulses were or might be channeled so as to add to personal strength and competence, and thus serve socially productive ends. By inquiring into the social and
developmental outcomes of everyday situations and
activities, Addams was able to bring both the experiential and the deliberately pedagogical aspects of education into view.

Addams also wrote often of formal education, and
placed a high priority on the improvement and the extension of public schooling. But she was convinced that
just as the full realization of democratic ideals would
require more than the granting of the franchise to all
citizens, so, too, would reliance upon education as a
basis for community, and hence for democracy, require
more than fuller opportunities for school learning. In
consequence, she could admire what she referred to
in an early speech as "the dream of transcendentalists
that each New England village would be a university,"
while also maintaining that study alone could not provide the active engagement in community concerns
that would foster the mutuality upon which real democracy had to be built.[2] Such mutuality required a
regard for others and an awareness of the necessity
of defining one's personal interests with reference to
collective, social interests, Addams believed; and as
she learned at Hull House, such mutuality could be
achieved only if culture and politics had vital meaning to all people.

Given these beliefs, it is not surprising that the reform of culture and politics became one of Jane Addams's preeminent goals. At Hull House, she rather
quickly became convinced of the importance of linking
culture and politics to popular wishes, needs, and activities. She decided, in other words, that culture and
politics would have greater value if they were related
to the contemporary experience of diverse groups of
people than they would if they were based solely on
classical or elite standards of beauty, conduct, and
morality. This early insight had a profound influence
on Addams's thought. It led her to argue and work for
fundamental changes in a great variety of institutions
as well as in many established patterns of belief. It led
her to hope that formal education could be organized
so as to contribute to the individual's capacity to engage with others in community affairs, thereby identi-
fying and advancing the common interests that would
foster gradual yet continuous social reform.

It was as a result of her experience at Hull House
that Jane Addams became a student of democracy and
of education. The entire corpus of her writings is significant for many reasons. Those of her writings that
deal with education may be most valuable for the clar-
ity with which they suggest the range of experiences
from which education may be derived. Even more,
perhaps, than did John Dewey, Jane Addams came
to see ever more clearly that schooling should be, not
an end in itself, but a means to other, broader educational opportunities. She believed that individually
and socially enhancing life experiences were the vital
sources and telling marks of a society in which democracy was a way of life, and not merely a rhetoric
or a political creed. It was a desire to find educational

opportunities of this broad experiential kind for herself and for others that took Addams to Hull House
in the first place and that desire continued to give direction to her thought.

II

How, then, did Jane Addams acquire the interests,
ideals, and ethical commitments, as well as the social
capacities, intellectual skills, and personal ambitions,
that were evident, first, in her move to Hull House
and, then, in her ability to formulate from her experience there a highly empirical social philosophy that
was at once original and rooted in the circumstances
of her day? At least in part, the answer lies in the education she herself received at home and in college and
from the study, travel, and seemingly aimless living
that marked her immediate postcollege years.

Jane Addams was twenty-nine years old when Hull
House was established. She was born on September
6, 1860, in Cedarville, a small, northern Illinois town
not far from Freeport. Her parents had migrated there
from Pennsylvania sixteen years earlier and had pros-
pered. Her father, John Huy Addams, a miller by
trade, had quickly become a prominent citizen. He
was a founder of many community institutions — the
church, the school, the library, and even the ceme-
tery — as well as a leading subscriber to the first railroad, which he had helped to bring to Cedarville. In
addition, he was one of the organizers and the first
president of the Second National Bank of Freeport.
A Whig who turned Republican when that party was

formed in 1854, he also served in the state senate for sixteen years.

As a child, Jane Addams was aware of her family's standing. She knew that her family's two-story, brick house was unusually large. And she knew, more importantly, that her father was a "dignified person," a "fine man."[3] Of her mother Jane could be equally proud, though Sarah Weber Addams died when Jane was two. She had responded to a call to help deliver a neighbor's baby—having herself borne eight children (four of whom died)—even though she was again pregnant at the time. On the way home, she had fallen and gone into premature labor. The baby had died within minutes of birth, and Sarah Addams, within a week. Although Jane Addams did not write of the circumstances surrounding her mother's death, she had a vague memory of the event and knew that her mother had been described in an obituary as a woman "with a heart ever alive to the wants of the poor," who would be "missed everywhere, at home, in society, in the church, in all places *where good is to be done and suffering relieved.*"[4]

If knowledge of her mother's character helped to mold Jane Addams's character, intimate acquaintance with her father's personality and values was certainly a source for all that she would be. Many of the recollections she included in *Twenty Years at Hull-House*, her first autobiography, were tinged with an interest in developing a logical plot line for her life. One must be skeptical, therefore, of certain of her claims—such as the one that, at the age of seven, in response to the sight of the "horrid little houses" surrounding her father's mill, she became determined that when she grew up she would have "a large house . . . in the midst of horrid little houses."[5] Possible retrospective embellishments notwithstanding, Addams's recollections convey a strong sense of connection to her father that is entirely believable, largely because her memories of her childhood are so incisively embroidered with commentary on the sources of his educational influence over her.

Having lost her mother and come to adore her father, who seems also to have adored her, Jane Addams apparently took her father as her chief childhood model. Imitation is the "sincere tribute . . . which affection offers its adored object," she observed in *Twenty Years at Hull-House*. She had "centered upon" her father, she explained, "all that careful imitation which a little girl ordinarily gives to her mother's ways and habits." Not surprisingly, therefore, the welcome she later extended to all people at Hull House was not different from the welcome her father had extended to her as an "ugly, pigeon-toed little girl, whose crooked back obliged her to walk with her head held very much upon one side." Having taken herself to be so misshapen (a perception others had not shared), she had been unable to "endure the thought that 'strange people' should know that my handsome father owned this homely little girl." But her father had not joined in her fear. One day, when he had gone out of his way to acknowledge their relationship in a crowded street—"with a playful touch of exaggeration, he lifted his high and shining silk hat and made me an imposing bow"—she happily saw "the absurdity of the entire feeling."[6]

John Addams's example also encouraged his daughter to study zealously as a young girl. "I was consumed by a wistful desire to apprehend the hardships of my father's earlier life," she wrote later. As her father had done as a miller's apprentice, she therefore spent the early hours of each day reading. She wanted to "understand life as he did."[7] The intellectual habits that were established in this way would subsequently be no less important than the social sympathies that similarly resulted from the modeling and imitation between father and daughter that was a constant feature of Jane Addams's early life.

Of course, John Huy Addams also shaped his daughter by means other than example. Jane Addams remembered going to her father with all her "sins and perplexities" and recalled with affection the gentleness with which he always interpreted her concerns. Through open, matter-of-fact interchange, John Addams shared with her his beliefs about equality and freedom and the commonalities that could exist between people of different nations. He helped her to understand that "you must always be honest with yourself inside." And he trained her to see the importance of individual conduct to the realization of one's espoused ideals.[8]

John Addams was not the only important person in Jane Addams's childhood. She had three older sisters (one of whom died at the age of sixteen), an older brother, and after 1868, when John Addams married Anna Haldeman of Freeport, a strong, beautiful, somewhat domineering, ambitious, and cultivated stepmother. James Weber Linn, Jane Addams's nephew and biographer, wrote that Anna Haldeman Addams "was what in those days was called 'accomplished.'"[9] She played the guitar and the piano and was a voracious reader. She brought a new style to the Cedarville household —

elegant furniture, silver for daily meals, more frequent visitors, witty conversation, and dramatic readings from Shakespeare. She offered her youngest stepdaughter constant tutelage in the social graces and cultural pursuits that were so much a part of late-Victorian definitions of "the lady."

Anna Haldeman Addams also brought her two sons to Cedarville after her marriage. Harry, the elder son, subsequently married one of Jane Addams's older sisters; George, the younger, became Jane's constant companion. A bright and adventuresome boy, George Haldeman helped Jane learn to play. A serious student who was fascinated by biology, he also interested her in nature study and science. From Anna Haldeman Addams, Jane gained a lasting appreciation for music and art; with George Haldeman, she experienced what she would later describe as "the companionship which children establish with nature . . . [an] identification with man's primitive life and . . . with the remotest past."[10] Even more than her relationships with her Addams siblings, those with her stepmother and stepbrother had an enduring impact on her, but neither was as educationally or emotionally significant as the relationship she had with her father. It was primarily from her father that Jane Addams acquired strength of character, moral idealism, and an inclination for a deliberate life.

This inclination was already apparent when, reaching the age of seventeen, Addams decided that she would go to Smith College in Northampton, Massachusetts. Smith was one of the new Eastern women's colleges. It opened in 1875, and like Vassar (which was founded in 1861) and Wellesley (which also opened

in 1875), it offered women a collegiate education similar to the education men could receive at colleges like
Yale, Princeton, and Harvard. Smith awarded the
bachelor's degree and in the eyes of many was regarded as a daring and risky experiment. In the year after
it was founded, Edward H. Clarke, a Harvard Medical
School professor, published a study called *Sex in Education* that heightened the controversy already surrounding the advisability of higher education for women.
Going beyond arguments concerning the irrelevance
of higher education to a woman's capacity to fulfill her
"natural" and socially sanctioned roles as a wife,
mother, teacher, and nurse—an exemplar of selfless
service and virtue at home and abroad—Clarke argued
that the mental exertion necessary for collegiate study
would cause women to break down, physically and
emotionally, and might even lead to sterility.[11]

In spite of arguments such as Clarke's, John Addams
favored advanced study for women, although he did
not concur in his daughter's decision to go to Smith.
Rather, he insisted that she go to Rockford Seminary,
which was close to the town of Cedarville and of which
he was a trustee. Originally chartered by the Presbyterian and Congregational conventions to offer academic and religious training to young women in the
upper Mississippi valley, Rockford resembled Mount
Holyoke Seminary (founded by Mary Lyon and opened
in 1837) in that the standards it maintained were more
like those of an academy than those of a men's college, the difference being that the standards of a men's
college were more uniformly rigorous and classics-ori-
ented than those of an academy. But Jane Addams's
older sisters had studied at Rockford, and, as a result,

despite her continuing wish to go to Smith, she was enrolled at the seminary as a freshman in the fall of 1877.

During her four years there she studied Greek, Latin, German, geology, astronomy, botany, medieval history, civil government, music, American literature, Bible, evidence of Christianity, and moral philosophy, as well as taking part in debating and literary activities and in the seminary's daily rounds of work and prayer, which were modeled on those of Mount Holyoke. In addition, she quickly became a leader among the approximately fifty other young women who were enrolled at Rockford at the time. A classmate remembered that "we never speculated as to why we liked to go to her room so that it was always crowded when the sacred 'engaged' sign was not hung out. We just knew that there was something 'doing' where she was, and that however mopey it might be elsewhere there was intellectual ozone in her vicinity."[12]

Most important of all, though, it was at Rockford that Jane Addams began to express considerable independence of mind and to articulate an aspiration to pursue feminist ideals. More than many of her peers, Addams was determined to resist the intense pressures to have a religious conversion that were still pervasive at the seminary, which for all intents and purposes was still a training school for missionaries. She therefore found subtle ways to disagree with and even to oppose the rigid and zealously religious headmistress, Anna P. Sill, who, Addams claimed, "does everything for people merely from love of God, and that I do not like."[13] As the speaker for the class of 1881 at their Junior Exhibition, the first such celebration in the seminary's history, Addams announced:

The fact of its being the first, seems to us a significant one, for it undoubtedly points more or less directly to a movement which is gradually claiming the universal attention. We mean the change which has taken place during the last fifty years in the ambition and aspirations of woman; we see this change most markedly in her education. It has passed from accomplishments and the arts of pleasing, to the development of her intellectual force, and capabilities for direct labor. She wishes not to be a man, nor like a man, but she claims the same right to independent thought and action . . . . As young women of the 19th century, we gladly claim these privileges, and proudly assert our independence, on the other hand we still retain the old ideal of womanhood. . . . So we have planned to be 'Bread-givers' throughout our lives; believing that in labor alone is happiness, and that the only true and honorable life is one filled with good works and honest toil, we have planned to idealize our labor, and thus happily fulfill Woman's Noblest Mission.[14]

Addams's speech, though avowing traditional notions of female service, challenged the conventional views of educational purpose held by the redoubtable "Miss Sill." It said nothing of piety and it claimed autonomy and independent thought as appropriate educational goals for women.

The habit of study that Jane Addams first developed in imitation of her father's systematic reading enabled her to excel academically at Rockford. And the tendency to self-direction, also nurtured by her father's example and teaching, enabled her to select for herself from among the ideals she was offered those she would, and would not, accept as her own. Like others of her classmates, Addams was plagued at times by questions of purpose. "That one should study, that one went to college for that purpose, was to our unsophisticated minds a simple self-evident fact, not debatable," a friend wrote of a group of which Jane Addams was a part. "Our only problem was study to what end?"[15] Such uncertainties notwithstanding, it was at Rockford that Addams began at least vaguely to identify what she wanted from life. While still a student there, Addams wrote to her close friend Ellen Gates Starr, who had left the seminary after a year to become a teacher, first in Mt. Morris, Illinois, and then at the Kirkland School for Girls in Chicago: "There is something in being in a big city, in giving somewhat as well as taking all the time, in gaining the ability not to move in ruts, that will give a self-reliance and an education a good deal better than a boarding school will."[16] Equally telling was her announcement in her senior essay that what women needed to gain was "what the ancients called *auethoritas* [sic], right of speaker to make themselves heard. . . . Let her not sit and dreamily watch her child," she wrote. "Let her work her way to a sentient idea that shall sway and ennoble those around her."[17]

At Rockford Jane Addams obviously began to formulate the ambitions she would finally act upon when she moved to Hull House and to recognize the sense of identity and destiny with other women that would serve as a continuing theme of her social criticism. But the seminary did not prepare Addams for a suitable adult role or satisfy her intellectual hunger. After graduation she continued to consider enrolling at Smith College. To go to Smith would signify even greater independence of action and even further commitment to the development of "intellectual force" than had four years at Rockford; and that accomplishment, recognized with the bachelor of arts degree, would be a further step toward the achievement of an authoritative, as opposed to a submissive and pleasing, woman's voice.

Jane Addams never did go to Smith, however. (She ultimately received the bachelor of arts degree from Rockford when that institution began granting such degrees in 1882.) When she returned to Cedarville after graduation, her father and stepmother still opposed her plan to study in the East; and in August of 1881, while on a trip to northern Wisconsin with his wife and Jane, John Addams died suddenly of a ruptured appendix. For eight years thereafter, his daughter endured bouts of deep depression and ill health, and was, for the time being, paralyzed in her ability to act on her previously formed ambitions.

During those eight years, Addams read Ruskin, Tolstoy, Goethe, George Eliot, and Hawthorne. She studied art and architecture, French and German. She took two extended tours of Europe, served as a companion to her stepmother, and helped to care for her nieces and nephews. For a brief time, she attended the Woman's Medical College in Philadelphia, but gave up the effort because of severe back trouble. Her stepbrother George Haldeman proposed marriage, but Jane refused him. She regarded George as a valued friend, but not as a potential husband; and doubtless, too, she was aware, as were other early women college graduates (fewer of whom married than did non-college women), that marriage would end all hopes for a life of more than traditional feminine concerns.

Only intermittently during this period did Addams

marshall the energy and interest that had been so much in evidence during her college years. The children at a Baltimore mission where she worked for a brief time stirred her, as did the poverty she observed in Europe. She enjoyed writing frequent soul-searching letters to Ellen Gates Starr and keeping a journal. She immersed herself in art, even falling "in love with the gothic" on her second trip to Europe.[18] And in May of 1888, she excitedly left the continent for London to attend the World Centennial Congress of Foreign Missions. While there, she read *The Children of Gibeon* and *All Sorts and Conditions of Men*, two Walter Besant novels in which wealthy women devote their lives and fortunes to the poor; she visited the workshops and classes of the People's Palace; and she met Canon Samuel A. Barnett, who had established a mission in the Whitechapel section of London in 1884.

Called Toynbee Hall, Barnett's mission was unusual. It served as a place of residence and work for Oxford men, rather than for Church of England clergymen. It resonated with the ideas of John Ruskin, who was then lecturing at Oxford, as well as with those of the (Marxist) Social Democratic Federation, William Morris's Socialist League, and the Fabian Society. As a living shrine to liberal versions of the social gospel, which linked social reform to religious duty, Toynbee Hall had become a frequent stopping place for young American idealists. By 1888, it had already helped to inspire Stanton Coit, an Amherst graduate, to establish the Neighborhood Guild (later renamed the University Settlement) in New York, and Vida Scudder, Jean Fine, and Helen Rand, all Smith graduates, to establish the College Settlement Association, which eventually sponsored settlements in New York, Boston, and Philadelphia.[19] Jane Addams described Toynbee Hall as "a community for University men who live there, have their recreation and clubs and society all among the poor people, yet in the same style [as] they would live in their own circle." Its attraction was tremendous. "It is so free from 'professional doing good,'" she wrote, "so unaffectedly sincere and so productive of good results in its classes and libraries so that it seems perfectly ideal."[20]

From London, Jane Addams wrote with verve to her sister of her interest in missions. Soon thereafter, she convinced Ellen Gates Starr to join with her in a plan to establish a settlement in Chicago. Fourteen months later, the two took up residence in the old mansion on Halstead and Polk Streets that would become Hull House. The decision to establish a settlement ended Addams's despond. It brought into clearer focus all that she had learned at home, at Rockford, and in Europe. It helped her clarify her religious stand; and it enabled her to see a way in which she might combine her wish to be of service to others — a "Bread-giver" — with her equally urgent wish to use and to gain influence — authority — through the powers of her mind.

Although she had managed to withstand Anna P. Sill's efforts to win her conversion and had not worried over theological matters to the extent that Ellen Gates Starr and others of her Rockford peers had done both before and after graduation, Jane Addams was nevertheless a religious person and was concerned about her lack of firm religious faith. Church services had been a constant feature of her childhood, and spiritual queries had been among the "sins and perplexi-

ties" with which she had so earnestly approached her
father, who, as she well knew, had been a deeply de-
vout if rather private and personally guided believer.
Religious questions concerning the meaning of faith,
the nature of afterlife, and the definition of sin, holi-
ness, and love had also suffused all of the art and literature Addams had studied. Quite naturally, therefore, she had wanted to be a believer, although she
had not been able to reconcile that wish with her deter-
mination to follow her father's admonition to "always
be honest with yourself inside." But in London, at
Toynbee Hall, she saw what religion could mean, not
as inherited dogma or abstract faith, but as a source
for a truly liberating social and personal creed.

Years before her visit to Toynbee Hall, Addams had
written to Starr: "You long for a beautiful faith, an
experience. . . . I only feel that I need religion in a
practical sense, that if I could fix myself with my relations to God and the universe, and so be in perfect
harmony with nature and deity, I could use my faculties and energy so much better and could do almost
anything."[21] The social gospel that was preached and
practiced at Toynbee Hall allowed her to do that. In
1885, after her first trip to Europe, Addams had joined
the Presbyterian church in Cedarville, although she
seems to have done so without sure, deep, personal
commitment. However that may be, in deciding to
open a settlement Addams embraced religion. During the early years at Hull House, her speeches were
filled with allusions to "salvation" and "Christ's message"; and just before moving there, she went so far
as to say that in comparison to a College Settlement
Association settlement she hoped that Hull House

would be "more distinctively Christian and less Social Science."[22] Statements such as these may indicate that Addams had not yet learned to express her moral commitments without reference to conventional religious terminology, or that she was, at least for a time, religious in a doctrinal sense. Regardless, by putting to rest the question of whether she was or was not a believer, Addams freed herself to ask the questions that would eventually lead her to enduring conviction: to the belief that religion was a matter of ethics and discipline, a means of aligning individual private action with the ever changing requirements of social need.

In deciding to establish a settlement, Addams also resolved the occupational dilemma she had wrestled with for at least eight years. In college, she had yearned for the right to freedom of expression, but had never gone so far as to demand access to traditionally male occupations. To be sure, after graduation she had considered a career in medicine, but she had given that up and had neither found, nor, more importantly, actively sought, an alternative profession. To have done so would have been difficult. Most college women of Addams's generation married and devoted themselves to domestic duties. Those who did not tended to go into teaching. Even at the turn of the century, only some 6 percent of the nation's medical students, 2 percent of its theological students, and 1 percent of its law students were women.[23] Statistics aside, Addams seems to have wanted a different kind of challenge than she would have been likely to find in an established profession. She had refused a chance to teach at Rockford. She was disinclined to provoke direct confrontation with convention, which entrance into a "male" profession would almost certainly have brought. She was searching for challenge, but not for the challenge of a learned craft. What Jane Addams wanted was a demanding, socially valuable, and stimulating way of life.

Marion Talbot, a founder of the Association of Collegiate Alumnae, who later became dean of women at the University of Chicago, wrote in 1931 that a college woman of the 1880s had to determine after graduation how best to "fit herself into her community and play the part in its life and program which was at once her interest and evident obligation."[24] Her statement reflected the frustration she and others had felt as they struggled to surmount a disarticulation between their college experiences and their postcollege opportunities. Addams, too, had suffered from this situation, but beginning with her visit to London in 1888, she began to see a way out of the problem she shared with other women of her social status and educational background. In the urban slum, there were people suffering from squalor, poverty, and disease—people with what Addams later called "objective" social need. Among college women like herself, there was also need, a "subjective" need for opportunities—educational opportunities—that would make it possible to relate learning to life. Somewhere, she sensed, there had to be a "fit" between the needs of these two different but not entirely dissimilar groups of people. Moreover, searching for that "fit" could in itself provide a vocation, and in turn would bring an end to the aimless living she so despised.

As a result of her visit to London, then, Addams

realized that she need not choose between existing vocational alternatives. She could reject both the possibility of a professional career and the possibility of a domestic career and still fulfill her wish for an independent, exciting, and socially responsible life. As was true of her discovery that there was a religion she could believe in, this insight was liberating. It enabled Addams to surmount the occupational dilemma that had previously stymied her. It transformed what had been the burden of unusual educational advantage into an opportunity for new experience. And it pointed Addams toward understanding that study unrelated to opportunities for work and service resulted in learning without instrumental value. In deciding to found a settlement, Addams recognized the social sources of a personal dilemma and in so doing was able to shift the focus of her thought and energy from self-analysis to the analysis of the society in which she lived. She had always been prone to severe self-criticism, as the negative and idiosyncratic self-image she had held as a child certainly showed; and she would always remain vulnerable to painful self-doubt — even going so far on one occasion as to wonder how she could have fallen so low, and become so different from her father, as to have been offered an unsolicited bribe. That notwithstanding, her recognition that other people, especially other young college women, had unmet needs and ambitions not different from her own enabled Jane Addams to overcome the paralysis that had resulted from her acute personal sensitivity and to begin to see that personal experience could and should be a source both for social inquiry and for social action.

III

Moving to Hull House was a happy and energizing turning point in Jane Addams's life. The move marked the culmination of a long and painful search and, in refocusing the questions that Addams could put to her experience, made it possible for her to continue her education in the broad experiential sense that she wrote of so well. It took time, though, and a good deal of observation, conversation, reading, and thought, before Addams would emerge as the settlement leader and social philosopher she would eventually be. The intellect, combined with down-to-earth practicality, sympathy, and shrewdness, that made Addams a leader among those of her contemporaries who also established or joined settlements — by 1900 there were more than 100 settlement houses in the United States and, by 1910, over 400 — were called forth by developments at Hull House, especially during the early years.[25]

When Hull House first opened, its activities were based on the presumption that life could be improved by sharing the advantages of learning with people who had not had the opportunities for study associated with a secure, American middle-class way of life. Acting on this presumption, Jane Addams and Ellen Gates Starr introduced themselves to their neighbors by inviting a number of neighborhood women to Hull House to hear them read George Eliot's novel *Romola*; and they continued, at first, to try to communicate in similarly quasi-didactic, quasi-philanthropic ways. The pleasure they felt when the reproductions of classical art that they lent were hung on tenement walls tells much about their initial belief in the value of "uplift."

Such presumptions notwithstanding, the Italian, Bohemian, Polish, and Russian Jewish immigrants who came to the settlement talked of their own interests and of their need for day care, health services, and garbage removal. Their requests made it clear to Addams that, if Hull House were to be the kind of neighborhood center she wanted it to be, sharing "culture" would not suffice. Over time, therefore, the Hull House program broadened, becoming less pretentious and more practical in its aims. Formal cultural and instructional activities did not disappear, but they were increasingly designed in a more collaborative fashion and were combined with efforts to investigate and alleviate neighborhood health, housing, and environmental problems. Writing of the program that had evolved by 1895, Jane Addams said: "All the details were left for the demands of the neighborhood to determine, and each department has grown from a discovery made through natural and reciprocal relations."[26]

Early developments at Hull House reflected Jane Addams's willingness to renounce the social and cultural sensibilities of her stepmother's set as well as her continuing recoil from the kind of single-minded missionizing that Anna P. Sill had exhibited at Rockford. They also reflected her renewed sense of connection with the example of her father. Indeed, the respectful humility and strength that Addams was to attribute to her father in *Twenty Years at Hull-House* were the very same qualities that were emerging in her as a result of her experience in Chicago. Most of all, however, the approach and the activities that began to take root at Hull House during the 1890s reflected the influence upon Jane Addams of the extraordinary circle of col-

leagues she found through her work. Addams's early
Hull House colleagues helped her to make sense of the
lives and problems of her neighbors and to put her
acute powers of observation and analysis to use in con-
veying to others the nature and social significance of
life in an urban, industrial, immigrant slum.

At the start, of course, Ellen Gates Starr was Addams's chief confidante and intellectual resource. The
two women had shared a close, supportive friendship
since 1877. But there were differences between them;
and, as other people joined them at Hull House, they
began to grow apart. Far more than Addams, Starr
was a person who found real solace in religion and who
relished the aesthetics of culture and craft. This is not
to say that she did not share Addams's social sympathies or that she drew back from political activism. In
fact, she was more likely than Addams to be found actually marching in a picket line with striking workers.
But Starr did tend to be more otherworldly than practical, and while she was increasingly drawn to the beauty of High Church Episcopalianism and to a Ruskin-
ian interest in art, Addams was increasingly drawn
to the more secular, hard-headed pragmatism that was
brought to Hull House by women like Julia Lathrop
and Florence Kelley.[27]

Lathrop came from an Illinois background much
like Addams's. She, too, had studied at Rockford, although she had gone on from there to Vassar and after college to read law in her father's law office while
serving as his clerk and secretary. She moved to Hull
House in 1890 and soon thereafter was made a member of the Illinois Board of Charities. Later on, she
helped to establish the first juvenile court and the Im-

migrants' Protection League. When the (federal) Children's Bureau was established in 1912, she became its first chief. In all these activities, Lathrop worked with Hull House residents, and throughout her life she and Addams remained close friends.[28]

Jane Addams claimed, in the biography she called *My Friend, Julia Lathrop*, that Julia Lathrop had "an unfailing sense of moral obligation and unforced sympathy" and that there were many stories she could tell that would show Lathrop's "disinterested virtue." Once, for example, she and Julia Lathrop were called to deliver the illegitimate baby of a neighbor whom no one else would help. Addams had apparently told Lathrop after the incident that she wondered if Hull House residents should let themselves be drawn into midwifery. Lathrop had responded with indignation. "If we have to begin to hew down to the line of our ignorance," she had said, "for goodness' sake don't let us begin at the humanitarian end. To refuse to respond to a poor girl in the throes of childbirth would be a disgrace to us forevermore. If Hull House does not have its roots in human kindness, it is no good at all."[29] In relating this story and others like it, Addams acknowledged that Lathrop had helped her to see that it was not for her to choose what services Hull House would offer. Hull House had to be ready to meet whatever needs its neighbors presented.

Florence Kelley also never let Addams forget the importance of responsiveness, although that was not her signal contribution either to Addams or to the settlement. According to James Weber Linn, who knew all the early residents at Hull House, Kelley was "the toughest customer in the reform riot, the finest rough-

and-tumble fighter for the good life for others, that
Hull-House ever knew."[30] By the time she moved to
Hull House in 1891, Kelley had been married, had
had three children, and was in the midst of a divorce.
More to the point, she was far more set in her views
than were the other residents.

A Quaker from Philadelphia who had graduated
from Cornell and studied at the University of Zurich,
Kelley was a socialist who believed in "the necessity
of applying the power of the *state* to prevent the modern
industrial system from destroying its own workers,
particularly women and children."[31] She had translated
Friedrich Engels's writings into English and worked in
Chicago as a special agent for the State Bureau of Labor Statistics before being appointed Chief Factory In-
spector by Governor John Peter Altgeld. By the time
she left Hull House in 1899 to become executive secretary of the National Consumers' League, the settlement was far more involved in industrial questions than
it had been earlier or, according to Addams, might ever
have become without Kelley. In addition, thanks to
Kelley Hull House became a center of social research.
Prone to tease Addams, as no one else dared to do
(though her son and others insisted that she "approved
of her unreservedly"), Kelley prodded Addams to re-
think her initial hope that the settlement should be
"more distinctively Christian and less Social Science."[32]
As Allen Davis has rightly argued, "more than any other
single person she was responsible for making Hull
House a center for reform, rather than a place to study
art and hear lectures on Emerson and Brook Farm."[33]

With Julia Lathrop, Florence Kelley also encouraged
Addams's emergence as a writer. Before Lathrop and

Kelley moved to Hull House, Addams had already begun her career as a public speaker, lecturing widely in and around Chicago to church groups and women's clubs. But it was in response to Lathrop's prodding that Addams sold her first two major articles — two talks she had given to the School of Applied Ethics in Plymouth, Massachusetts — which were published in the *Forum* in 1892. And it was through Kelley that Addams met Richard T. Ely, whom she referred to later as her "sociological grandfather."[34]

A well-known professor of economics, Ely played an important part in turn-of-the-century efforts to move economics and social science in general from abstraction to empiricism and from a conservative laissez-faire perspective to one that was more in line with reformist, Christian Socialist leanings. In addition to being active in the Chautauqua movement, he helped to found the American Economic Association and taught at Johns Hopkins University until he joined the faculty of the University of Wisconsin in 1892.[35] Hull House embodied many of the ideals Ely espoused. He was convinced and in turn convinced Kelley, who convinced Addams, that investigations at Hull House could result in a sociological survey on a par with Charles Booth's pioneering study of life in a London slum, which had been published in seventeen volumes between 1891 and 1903 as *Life and Labour of the People in London*. The outcome was *Hull-House Maps and Papers*, published in 1895. In addition, Ely arranged for Addams to lecture at the University of Wisconsin and then, in 1902, to have the lectures published as part of a Chautauqua adult education series. Entitled *Democracy and Social Ethics* and, according to her nephew, thought of by Addams as a sociological text, the lectures became her first book.

There were many other people during the early years at Hull House who played important roles in Addams's development. Among these, Mary Rozet Smith was especially significant for the emotional support she provided Addams within the context of a long-standing relationship of great closeness and mutual affection; and Louise de Koven Bowen was important, not only for the friendship she offered, but also for the money she gave to support new Hull House projects and buildings. Many faculty members from the University of Chicago (founded three years after Hull House opened) also found their way to the settlement, offering help with clubs and classes and, in some instances, educating Addams as she also educated them. George Herbert Mead, the psychologist who began the development of the field of social interactionism, became one of Addams's valued intellectual comrades. So too did sociologist W. I. Thomas, whose classic study *The Polish Peasant in Europe and America* (coauthored with Florian Znaniecki) helped to legitimate the scholarly use of personal documents. It was his famous dictum — "If men define situations as real, they are real in their consequences" — that helped to inaugurate inquiry into the sociology of knowledge.[36] In addition to Mead and Thomas, the educator and philosopher John Dewey became one of Addams's most notable and valued friends.

Dewey first visited Hull House in 1892 when he was considering leaving the University of Michigan to accept a position offered him by the first president of the University of Chicago, William Rainey Harper. Immediately thereafter, he wrote to Addams of his belief that she had "taken the right way." In the years that followed, he visited Hull House frequently, to participate in Julia Lathrop's Plato Club or simply to talk with Addams. When the settlement was incorporated in 1895, he became a member of its board of trustees, remarking later that he and the other trustees had served primarily to tell Addams, "You are all right: go ahead."[37]

The relationship that grew up between Addams and Dewey was enhanced by personal regard. Dewey's daughter Jane Mary Dewey was named for Jane Addams and Mary Rozet Smith, and Addams gave the memorial service address for Dewey's son Gordon, who died at the age of eight.[38] But the relationship was primarily based on a mutually influential exchange of ideas. Dewey's daughter claimed that her father's "faith in democracy as a guiding force in education took on both a sharper and deeper meaning because of Hull-House and Jane Addams."[39] And Addams claimed in turn that Dewey had provided her with philosophic insights that she found vital to the translation of her early intuitive beliefs into a more fully elaborated understanding of relationships between inquiry and action and personal and social ideals. He taught us "a method," she remarked in 1929. "In those years when we were told by the scientists, or at least by the so-called scientists, that the world was in the grasp of sub-human forces against which it was absurd to oppose the human will, John Dewey calmly stated that the proper home of intelligence was the world itself and that the true function of intelligence was to act as critic and regulator of the forces which move the world."[40]

Jane Addams's acquaintance grew with the years, and she learned a good deal from many different people as well as from her increasing involvement in Chicago politics and in reform causes throughout the nation and the world. Addams served on the Chicago School Board. She seconded Theodore Roosevelt's nomination as the presidential candidate of the Progressive Party in 1912. She was a member of the first executive committee of the National Association for the Advancement of Colored People, a vice-president of the National American Woman Suffrage Association, and a founder of the American Union Against Militarism, from which emerged both the Foreign Policy Association and the American Civil Liberties Union. She was elected chairman of the Woman's Peace Party in 1915, and in 1919 she became the first president of the Women's International League for Peace and Freedom, having presided over the 1915 International Congress of Women at The Hague from which the League originated.

All of these efforts, especially those for woman suffrage and international peace, found their way into Addams's writings. But it was of her experience at Hull House that she wrote most often and from her experience there that she derived her most profound insights into education. The life of her Hull House neighbors, filtered through the values and ideals of her childhood, always gave focus to what Jane Addams did and said. She had had a keen and well-trained mind when she moved to the settlement, and she had been eager to find ways to use it to serve others. But her capacity to understand the social implications of her own experience and that of others was greatly enhanced by the informal tutelage she received from her fellow workers, especially during the 1890s.

IV

After her move to Hull House, Jane Addams increasingly achieved public renown. Although she endured considerable hostility during World War I as a result of her pacifism, even being portrayed by some as a "red" radical of questionable loyalties, she was widely admired and respected throughout her career. During her early decades at Hull House, she was described by journalists as altruistic, benevolent, and kind; and after the militarist hysteria of the First World War had abated, and especially after she was awarded the Nobel Prize for Peace in 1931, she was frequently portrayed as a kind of secular saint. To many of her contemporaries, as to many people since, Jane Addams was female virtue and generosity incarnate, an "American heroine," the "benevolent lady."

Certainly deserved in some ways, Addams's reputation was nevertheless more stereotypic than accurate. Although she was, indeed, gentle, empathetic, and giving, she was also capable of great strength, even of toughness, and had a powerful mind. What is more, if she managed to identify and to meet "objective" social need, she also managed to recognize, analyze, and avow "the subjective necessity" for her actions. Finally, while deeply committed to effecting concrete, practical, and immediate improvements in the life circumstances of men, women, and children in Chicago and elsewhere, she was also committed to demonstrating

the role and power of ideas in promoting more fundamental and lasting social change.

Fully recognized and appreciated for her deeds and
for her goodness, Jane Addams was not equally recognized and appreciated for her ability to analyze and
criticize the society in which she lived. Her writings
were praised as incisive, but they were often reviewed
as the writings of a woman. "No other book by a woman shows such vitality, such masculinity of mental grasp
and surefootedness," the economist Edwin Seligman
said of *Democracy and Social Ethics* when it appeared in
1902. The jurist Oliver Wendell Holmes agreed. Jane
Addams is a "big woman who knows at least the facts,"
he wrote. She "gives me more insight into the point
of view of the working man and the poor than I had
before."[41]

Comments such as these, which today might suggest
overt and even purposeful gender-related discounting,
at the time primarily reflected the still pervasive influence of notions having to do with female capacities and
gender-distinct "spheres." From at least the early nineteenth century, it was generally assumed in the United
States that women had special nurturant qualities and
virtues, and that these made them especially able to
offer love, sympathy, comfort, and succor to members
of their families and others in need. Logically, in light
of this, a woman's "sphere" was presumed to encompass
only those worlds where the heart, as opposed to the
mind, was most needed. The home, the sickroom, the
elementary classroom, and other places where humane
services and tenderness were provided were considered
her special preserve. All this, as Jane Addams knew
full well, made "breadgiving" seem as "natural" for a

woman as it made the assertion of mind — authority — seem "unnatural." To the extent, then, that reviews of Addams's books tended to praise her achievements as not only rare but anomalous, they both reflected and perpetuated presumptions of "sphere."

If traditional interpretations of female capacities skewed interpretations of Jane Addams's work, magnifying its benevolent aspects while masking and demeaning its closely related intellectual side, so too, and equally significantly, did changing perceptions of what did and did not fall within the perimeters of legitimate social science. As a thinker, Addams was more like a nineteenth-century "amateur" social scientist than she was like a twentieth-century "professional" scholar. She subscribed to nineteenth-century convictions having to do with direct, causative relationships between social progress and the general dissemination of knowledge, although she added ideas that were both feminist and radical to this traditional rationale for social science.

Addams was convinced that public consciousness and public policies were integrally related, and she thought both were in need of fundamental change. They had to be suffused, she believed, with what she and her contemporaries of both sexes took to be female concerns — concerns about the health, welfare, and education of children and immigrants, the excluded and the poor. More important still, she insisted that closer links needed to be developed between inquiry and action. Only when inquiry and action were joined, Addams argued, would there be achieved a fuller, more overtly avowed, and actually lived recognition of the rootedness of social ethics in the individual conduct and ideals that defined personal experience. Only with thoroughgoing moral reform, she insisted, would changes in law and in economic and social institutions eventually result in greater justice and enfranchisement for all.

Jane Addams's understanding of the relationship that ought to exist between social need, social inquiry, and social action, as well as her view of the intellectual, institutional, and moral reorientation that would have to take place to achieve this, were not idiosyncratic at the turn of the century. Her views were shared by many other women, especially those who subscribed to a "social feminist consciousness"; and they were also shared by prominent male reformers and social scientists, including Richard T. Ely, her "sociological grandfather," and the University of Chicago faculty members who had been among her early Hull House colleagues.[42] During the 1890s, when the variety of reform impulses that slowly coalesced into the progressive movement were just beginning to be expressed, Addams's views enjoyed a relatively wide and androgynous support.

In the decades that followed, however, as the evangelicism and optimism of early progressive protest became increasingly intertwined with a respect, even a reverence, for science, expertise, and professionalism, Addams's views became more and more marginal and began to lose their earlier and wider cross-sex appeal. Much was involved in this change of attitude, the notable development of relevance to this discussion being the increasing acceptance of sociology, psychology, and other once-intertwined branches of social science as distinct, university-based, professional fields of scholarly research.

This trend toward specialization within social science

was nowhere more evident than at the University of Chicago. The university established the nation's first department of social science in 1892, including within it at the start sociology, anthropology, and a motley array of applied and reform-oriented subjects called "sanitary science." Then, in 1904, sanitary science was moved out of this department and placed in a newly created department of "household administration." At the same time, the university established training in social work.[43]

In addition to being the first in the nation, the Chicago department of social science was for many years paradigm setting. Developments at Chicago were widely influential. As a result, the new departmental lines drawn there created divisions, not just at Chicago, but also elsewhere, between theoretical, "objective," academic social research, on the one hand, and more reformist, political, and applied social work, on the other. The structural and intellectual divisions thus created were soon compounded by gender divisions that rapidly took on hierarchical status distinctions as well. Sociology, which came increasingly to be dominated by men, was more and more seen as a source for insights to be tested and applied by "social workers," most of whom were women; and settings for "social work," including social settlements like Hull House, were more and more seen as places to which (male) university sociologists might send students to collect data, which the sociologists and not the social workers would then analyze in a university laboratory and elaborate into theory.[44]

Early-twentieth-century developments in sociology, such as those at the University of Chicago, were not

dissimilar from roughly contemporaneous developments in other fields of social science, which for a time
had been areas of study that were relatively open to
women.[45] Such developments, when accompanied by
an increase in gender segregation in undergraduate
study, played a crucial role in introducing the notion
of gender-distinct spheres into the burgeoning early-
twentieth-century world of the university. The introduction and institutionalization within the university
of gender-distinct spheres and the transmission through
university teaching and research of expectations related
to these spheres reinforced more general expectations
about gender-related capacities, and thus helped further to define, and limit, the way in which Jane Addams's writings were received.[46] Although Addams
herself never fully concurred in the judgment, her
views became increasingly associated with the professional practice of female altruism — put otherwise, with
professional social work — and conversely, increasingly
disassociated from the professional study of sociology,
which was dominated and controlled, not only through
university departments, but also through journals and
the American Sociological Association, by men.[47]

In some ways, of course, this division lessened the
influence that Addams's writings might otherwise have
achieved. But the increasing fragmentation and professionalization of social science did not have only negative consequences for Addams's work. By isolating
Addams and other women reformers and social scientists, these developments helped to join them ever
more closely in informal female networks that sought
and achieved any number of significant policy innova-
tions, ranging from the establishment of the (federal)

Children's Bureau in 1912 to the passage of New Deal labor legislation.[48] Equally important, these trends may have had the somewhat ironic effect of enhancing Addams's ability to identify and articulate what she believed. At least during her early years at Hull House, much that she said about settlements and settlement work took the form of dissent from increasing admiration for abstract, "objective," scholarly knowledge. Thus, in an 1899 paper read before the American Academy of Political and Social Science, she presented the social settlement as a potential corrective to what she still called "the college:"

> As the college changed from teaching theology to teaching secular knowledge the test of its success should have shifted from the power to save men's souls to the power to adjust them in healthful relations to nature and their fellow men. But the college failed to do this, and made the test of its success the mere collecting and dissemination of knowledge, elevating the means into an end and falling in love with its own achievement.[49]

Similarly, in a 1904 speech on immigration delivered at the University of Chicago, through criticism of "the scholar" she implied what the settlement worker should do. Beginning with a polite nod to scholarly contributions to "the field," she went on to say:

> To let the scholar off with the mere collecting of knowledge, or yet with its transmission, or indeed to call his account closed with that still higher function of research, would be to throw away one of our most valuable assets. . . . The scholar has furnished us with no method by which to discover men, to spiritualize, to understand, to hold intercourse with aliens and to receive of what they bring.[50]

Statements such as these show that Jane Addams was
deeply concerned with formulating views of knowledge, research, and reform, as well as views of their
proper relation, that were in many ways different from
those that prevailed.

Because Jane Addams's writings embodied these
views and therefore pertained directly to the immediate circumstances of her world, they sometimes present particular situations and advocate specific changes
of policy that have little direct relevance to social problems today. But to let that detract from their more fundamental value would be to ignore their more essential
and enduring message. Jane Addams's writings assert
the belief that abstract social values like justice, freedom, equality, and peace are concretely defined by
daily actions and beliefs. They urge the possibility
that progress toward greater justice, fuller freedom,
more complete equality, and a lasting peace may be
achieved, if, through social experimentation, study,
and discussion, men and women become ever more
cognizant of the shared consequences and social aspects of their lives. Addams's writings are those of a
moralist and an idealist: of a person who never doubt-
ed that there could be values upon which all people
would agree, and who never renounced the conviction
that ideas might lessen and in time even modify the
pervasiveness and debilitating effects of poverty, pow-
erlessness, and social class. Addams's writings may be
criticized for the biases they reveal, but they pose a
key question of liberal, democratic social philosophy:
the question of how, through education and experience, all people can be more fully empowered to pursue their separate, reciprocal, and common goals. It
is the significance of that question as well as the as-

tuteness of her reflections upon it that make Jane Addams's writings worth reading still.

NOTES

1. This description of the Hull House program is taken from Jane Addams, "Hull-House: A Social Settlement," appendix in *Hull-House Maps and Papers* (New York: Thomas Y. Crowell, 1895), pp. 207–230. Later descriptions may be found in Jane Addams, *Twenty Years at Hull-House* (New York: Macmillan, 1910) and *The Second Twenty Years at Hull-House* (New York: Macmillan, 1930).

2. Jane Addams, "The Subjective Necessity for Social Settlements," in *Philanthropy and Social Progress*, ed. Henry C. Adams (Thomas Y. Crowell, 1893), p. 8.

3. Addams, *Twenty Years at Hull-House*, p. 7.

4. Quoted in James Weber Linn, *Jane Addams: A Biography* (New York: D. Appleton-Century, 1935), pp. 22–23.

5. Addams, *Twenty Years at Hull-House*, pp. 3–5.

6. Addams, *Twenty Years at Hull-House*, pp. 11–12, 7–9.

7. Addams, *Twenty Years at Hull-House*, pp. 12–13.

8. Addams, *Twenty Years at Hull-House*, pp. 13 and 15.

9. Linn, *Jane Addams*, p. 30.

10. Addams, *Twenty Years at Hull-House*, pp. 17–18.

11. Edward H. Clarke, *Sex in Education; or, A Fair Chance for the Girls* (Boston: J. R. Osgood, 1873). For a general discussion of the development of collegiate education for women as well as opposition to it see Thomas Woody, *A History of Women's Education in the United States*, 2 vols. (1929; reprint, New York: Octagon Books, 1966), vol. 2, chap. 4.

12. Quoted in Linn, *Jane Addams*, p. 47.

13. Quoted in Allen F. Davis, *American Heroine: The Life and Legend of Jane Addams* (New York: Oxford University Press, 1973), p. 14.

14. Jane Addams, "Bread Givers," *Rockford Daily Register*, April 21, 1880; reprinted in *Jane Addams: A Centennial Reader* (New York: Macmillan, 1960), pp. 103–104.

15. Quoted in Linn, *Jane Addams*, p. 51.

16. Quoted in Davis, *American Heroine*, p. 14.

17. Quoted in Davis, *American Heroine*, p. 22.

18. Quoted in Davis, *American Heroine*, p. 48.

19. Allen F. Davis, *Spearheads for Reform: The Social Settlements and the Progressive Movement 1890–1914* (New York: Oxford University Press, 1967), pp. 8–14.

20. Quoted in Davis, *American Heroine*, p. 49.

21. Quoted in Davis, *American Heroine*, p. 17.

22. Quoted in John C. Farrell, *Beloved Lady: A History of Jane Addams' Ideas on Reform and Peace* (Baltimore: Johns Hopkins University Press, 1967), p. 61.

23. Woody, *A History of Women's Education*, vol. 2, pp. 360, 369, and 370.

24. Quoted in Joyce Antler, "The Educated Woman and Professionalization: The Struggle for a New Feminine Identity, 1890–1920" (Ph.D. diss., State University of New York at Stony Brook, 1977), pp. 137–138.

25. Davis, *Spearheads for Reform*, p. 12.

26. Addams, "Hull-House: A Social Settlement," pp. 208.

27. *Notable American Women*, s.v. "Starr, Ellen Gates."

28. *Notable American Women*, s.v. "Lathrop, Julia Clifford."

29. Jane Addams, *My Friend, Julia Lathrop* (New York: Macmillan, 1935), pp. 49 and 53.

30. Linn, *Jane Addams*, pp. 138–139.

31. Linn, *Jane Addams*, p. 137.

32. Linn, *Jane Addams*, p. 138.

33. Davis, *American Heroine*, p. 77. For Kelley's life see *Notable American Women*, s.v. "Kelley, Florence"; Dorothy Rose Blumberg, *Florence Kelley: The Making of a Social Pioneer* (New York: Augustus M. Kelley, 1966); and Josephine Goldmark, *Impatient Crusader: Florence Kelley's Life Story* (Urbana: University of Illinois Press, 1953).

34. Quoted in Davis, *American Heroine*, p. 102.

35. Richard T. Ely, *Ground Under Our Feet: An Autobiography* (New York: Macmillan, 1938).

36. Mary Jo Deegan and John S. Burger, "George Herbert Mead and Social Reform: His Work and Writings," *Journal of the History of the Behavioral Sciences* 14 (1978): 362–373; and "W. I. Thomas and Social Reform: His Work and Writings," *Journal of the History of the Behavioral Sciences* 17 (1981): 114–125.

37. Quoted in Davis, *American Heroine*, pp. 97 and 109.

38. Jane Addams, "Gordon Dewey," in *The Excellent Becomes the Permanent* (New York: Macmillan, 1932), pp. 61–69.

39. Jane M. Dewey, "Biography of John Dewey," in *The Philosophy of John Dewey*, ed. Paul Arthur Schilpp, 2d ed. (La Salle, Ill.: Open Court Publishing, 1951), p. 30.

40. Jane Addams, "A Toast to John Dewey," *Survey* 63 (1929): 203–204.

41. Both reviews are quoted in Davis, *American Heroine*, p. 128.

42. Ellen Condliffe Lagemann, *A Generation of Women: Education in the Lives of Progressive Reformers* (Cambridge, Mass.: Harvard University Press, 1979), pp. 154–160; Benjamin G. Rader, *The Academic Mind and Reform: The Influence of Richard T. Ely in American Life* (Lexington: University of Kentucky Press, 1966), pp. 28–129; and Rosalind Rosenberg, *Beyond Separate Spheres: Intellectual Roots of Modern Feminism* (New Haven: Yale University Press, 1982), pp. 28–53.

43. Steven J. Diner, "Department and Discipline: The Department of Sociology at the University of Chicago, 1892–1920," *Minerva* 13 (1975): 514–553; and Rosenberg, *Beyond Separate Spheres*, pp. 43–51. Social work training began in 1903 in the Institute of Social Science; was reorganized under the auspices of the School of Civics and Philanthropy in 1907; and was finally transferred to the School of Social Service Administration in 1920.

44. Rosenberg, *Beyond Separate Spheres*; and Mary Jo Deegan, "Women in Sociology: 1890–1920," *Journal of the History of Sociology* 1 (1978): 11–34.

45. Rosenberg, *Beyond Separate Spheres*; Margaret W. Rossiter, *Women Scientists in America: Struggles and Strategies to 1940* (Baltimore: Johns Hopkins University Press, 1982); and Dorothy Ross, "The Development of the Social Sciences," in *The Organization of Knowledge in Modern America 1860–1920*, ed. Alexandra Oleson and John Voss (Baltimore: Johns Hopkins University Press, 1979), pp. 107–138.

46. Ellen Condliffe Lagemann, "Looking at Gender: Women's History," in *Historical Inquiry in Education*, ed. John Hardin Best (Washington, D.C.: American Educational Research Association, 1983), pp. 251–264.

47. Addams believed that social work embodied natural, historically female concerns, a belief that led her to suffragism (see,

for example, Jane Addams, "Woman Suffrage and the Protection of the Home," *Ladies' Home Journal* 27 [1910]: 21, as well as comments throughout *Newer Ideals of Peace* [New York: Chautauqua Press, 1970]). She saw formal training for social work as an advantage that her "pre-efficiency" generation had not had: Jane Addams, "How Much Social Work Can a Community Afford: From the Ethical Point of View," *Proceedings of the National Conference of Social Work* (1926), pp. 108–109. She also feared, however, that the natural, emotional, and ethical aspects of social work might be lost with increasing professionalization: Linn, *Jane Addams*, pp. 111–112; and Farrell, *Beloved Lady*, p. 139. On the isolation of women sociologists from their male colleagues see Mary Jo Deegan, "Early Women Sociologists and the American Sociological Society: The Patterns of Exclusion and Participation," *American Sociologist* 16 (1981): 14–24.

48. Nancy P. Weiss, "The Children's Bureau: A Case Study in Women's Voluntary Networks" (Paper delivered at the Second Berkshire Conference on the History of Women, Bryn Mawr, Pennsylvania, 10 June 1976); and Susan Ware, *Beyond Suffrage: Women in the New Deal* (Cambridge, Mass.: Harvard University Press, 1981).

49. Jane Addams, "A Function of the Social Settlement," *Annals of the American Academy of Political and Social Science* 13 (1899): 339–340.

50. Jane Addams, "Recent Immigration, a Field Neglected by Scholars," *University Record* (Chicago) 9 (1905): 246–247.

Bibliographic Essay

Jane Addams was a prolific writer. She published eleven major books: *Democracy and Social Ethics* (New York: Macmillan, 1902); *Newer Ideals of Peace* (New York: Macmillan, 1907); *The Spirit of Youth and the City Streets* (New York: Macmillan, 1909); *Twenty Years at Hull-House* (New York: Macmillan, 1910); *A New Conscience and an Ancient Evil* (New York: Macmillan, 1912); (with Emily G. Balch and Alice Hamilton) *Women at The Hague, The International Congress of Women and Its Results* (New York: Macmillan, 1915); *The Long Road of Woman's Memory* (New York: Macmillan, 1916); *Peace and Bread in Time of War* (New York: Macmillan, 1922); *The Second Twenty Years at Hull-House* (New York: Macmillan, 1930); *The Excellent Becomes the Permanent* (New York: Macmillan, 1932); and *My Friend, Julia Lathrop* (New York: Macmillan, 1935). She also published some five hundred articles, often including the same material in more than one piece. John C. Farrell, *Beloved Lady: A History of Jane Addams's Ideas on Reform and Peace* (Baltimore: Johns Hopkins University Press, 1967), contains a chronological bibliography indicating those articles that are reprints or excerpts of earlier material. An even fuller bibliography that includes archival sources (most of Addams's papers are at Hull-House in Chicago or at the Swarthmore College Peace Collection), magazine and newspaper accounts, and other secondary sources is Helen M. Perkins, comp., *A Preliminary Checklist for a Bibli-*

ography on Jane Addams (Rockford, Ill.: Jane Addams
Centennial Committee, 1960).

On the centennial of Addams's birth, the Women's
International League for Peace and Freedom published
a collection of excerpts from her writings, *Jane Addams:
A Centennial Reader* (New York: Macmillan, 1960), that
is organized by category. Education is not listed as a
category, although some of Addams's educational writings appear. Each topic is introduced by a brief essay
assessing Addams's contribution to the particular field.
Christopher Lasch, ed., *The Social Thought of Jane Addams* (Indianapolis: Bobbs-Merrill, 1965), is another
general collection that begins with a brief but excellent
essay in which Lasch describes Addams as a "theorist
and intellectual — a thinker of originality and daring"
(p. xv). Allen F. Davis, ed., *Jane Addams on Peace, War,
and International Understanding 1899–1932* (New York:
Garland, 1976), is a more specialized anthology. While
no collection can substitute for reading Addams's writings in full, all of these are valuable for placing Addams's educational writings within the context of her
writings on other questions, especially suffragism, pacifism, and internationalism, which were her major interests from World War I until her death.

A knowledge of Addams's life is important for an
understanding of her thought, and fortunately there
are many biographies to supplement the autobiographical record she provided in *Twenty Years at Hull-House*
and *The Second Twenty Years at Hull-House*. There are
entries on Addams in the *Dictionary of American Biography*
and in *Notable American Women*, the latter entry having
been written by Anne Firor Scott, whose introduction
to the John Harvard Library edition of *Democracy and
Social Ethics* (Cambridge, Mass.: Harvard University

Press, 1964) further describes Addams's life in relation to changing female roles. The earliest full biography is James Weber Linn, *Jane Addams: A Biography* (New York: D. Appleton-Century, 1935). Linn was Addams's nephew, and his biography includes personal memories of Addams and Hull-House as well as much otherwise unavailable family lore. Even though it is more descriptive than critically interpretative, the book provides a useful portrait and has served as a source for most subsequent accounts. John C. Farrell, *Beloved Lady: A History of Jane Addams's Ideas on Reform and Peace*, is a complete and thoughtful intellectual biography. Daniel Levine, *Jane Addams and the Liberal Tradition* (Madison: State Historical Society of Wisconsin, 1971), describes her contribution to social reform. Allen F. Davis, *American Heroine: The Life and Legend of Jane Addams* (New York: Oxford University Press, 1973), is the best full-length treatment of her life, although Davis's argument that Addams had "a peculiar need to be reassured, [which] left her dependent on honors, awards, and public approval" (p. 39), along with his belief that this led her purposefully to cultivate the image of a "heroine," has been controversial.

In addition to these, there are many brief studies of Addams. Jill Conway, "Jane Addams: An American Heroine," *Daedalus* 93 (1964): 761–780, examines Addams's career in reference to changing attitudes toward women, and, if possible, should be read in conjunction with Jill Kathryn Conway, "The First Generation of American Women Graduates" (Ph.D. diss., Harvard University, 1968). Although J. O. C. Philips, "The Education of Jane Addams," *History of Education Quarterly* 14 (1974): 49–67, begins with an unfortunate question, "How did an ambitious egotistical woman in 19th

century America break through the incredibly limited
bonds which the domestic piety tradition had established for women" (p. 49), his account is rich in detail
and context. Christopher Lasch, "Jane Addams: *The
College Woman and the Family Claim*," in *The New Radi-
calism in America [1889–1963]: The Intellectual as a Social
Type* (New York: Alfred A. Knopf, 1966), pp. 3–37,
deals with Addams in connection with what Lasch sees
as the progressive revolt against the Victorian family.
Merle Curti, "Jane Addams on Human Nature," *Journal of the History of Ideas* 22 (1961): 240–253, and Daniel
Levine, "Jane Addams," in *Varieties of Reform Thought*
(Madison: State Historical Society of Wisconsin, 1964),
pp. 10–32, treat Addams's ideas, as does Paul C.
Violas, "Jane Addams and the New Liberalism," in
Roots of Crisis: American Education in the Twentieth Century,
ed. Clarence J. Karier, Paul C. Violas, and Joel Spring
(Chicago: Rand, McNally, 1973), pp. 66–83, where
Addams is presented as "a primary architect" of a "new
middle-class ideology" that fostered "acceptance of a
compulsory corporate state in which the individual
would be simply a part of the greater collective unity"
(p. 68). Violas's account explicitly disagrees with an
earlier treatment of Addams as an important proponent
of the democratization of culture that is set forth in
Lawrence A. Cremin, *The Transformation of the School:
Progressivism in American Education, 1876–1957* (New
York: Alfred A. Knopf, 1961). I find the latter interpretation more compatible with Addams's actual writings. Bettina Aptheker, "Lynching and Rape: An Exchange of Views by Jane Addams and Ida B. Wells,"
Occasional Paper No. 25 (San Jose: American Institute for Marxist Studies, 1977), analyzes Addams's

position on questions of race, concluding that, limitations in vision notwithstanding, Addams's "pro-civil rights activities were conspicuous" (p. 5).

There are many accounts of turn-of-the-century Chicago that deal with Jane Addams and Hull House, among them: Ray Ginger, *Altgeld's America: The Lincoln Ideal versus Changing Realities* (New York: Funk & Wagnalls, 1958); Helen Lefkowitz Horowitz, *Culture & the City: Cultural Philanthropy in Chicago from the 1880s to 1917* (Lexington: University Press of Kentucky, 1976); and Kathleen D. McCarthy, *Noblesse Oblige: Charity & Cultural Philanthropy in Chicago, 1849–1929* (Chicago: University of Chicago Press, 1982). Material on Addams may also be found in general works on the settlement movement: see, for example, Allen F. Davis, *Spearheads for Reform: The Social Settlements and the Progressive Movement 1890–1914* (New York: Oxford University Press, 1967) and Maureen Karen Fastenau, "Maternal Government: The Social Settlement Houses and the Politicization of Women's Sphere, 1889–1920" (Ph.D. diss., Duke University, 1982); and on reform campaigns that grew out of the settlement movement: Anthony M. Platt, *The Child Savers: The Invention of Delinquency* (Chicago: University of Chicago Press, 1969). In addition, there is a voluminous literature on progressivism. A recent example that includes a nice description of Addams is Robert M. Crunden, *Ministers of Reform: The Progressives' Achievement in American Civilization, 1889–1920* (New York: Basic Books, 1982), which revives Richard Hofstadter's classic "status revolution" argument (*The Age of Reform From Bryan to F.D.R.* [New York: Alfred A. Knopf, 1955], chap. 4), adding to it new scholarship on the evangelical tradition.

Because Jane Addams was a major figure in American social and intellectual history, there is a great deal of literature, encompassing richly diverse interpretations, to which one can turn in studying her. The works cited here may be useful as an initial guide.

1

The Subjective Necessity
for Social Settlements

*Addams always argued that a settlement was based on reciprocal
need: a need on the part of the poor for help with concrete, immediate, "objective" problems; and a need on the part of the
privileged for opportunities to translate ideals into action. Here,
in the first of two talks she gave at the School of Applied Ethics
in Plymouth, Massachusetts, in 1892, she describes the appeal of settlement work to educated young people like herself.*

Hull House, which was Chicago's first Settlement, was
established in September, 1889. It represented no association, but was opened by two women, backed by
many friends, in the belief that the mere foothold of
a house, easily accessible, ample in space, hospitable
and tolerant in spirit, situated in the midst of the large
foreign colonies which so easily isolate themselves in
American cities, would be in itself a serviceable thing
for Chicago. Hull House endeavors to make social intercourse express the growing sense of the economic
unity of society. It is an effort to add the social function to democracy. It was opened on the theory that
the dependence of classes on each other is reciprocal;

SOURCE: Henry C. Adams, ed., *Philanthropy and Social Progress*
(New York: Thomas Y. Crowell, 1893), pp. 1–26. Originally published as "A New Impulse to an Old Gospel," *Forum* 14 (1892):
342–356. Later included in *Twenty Years at Hull-House* (New York:
Macmillan, 1910), chap. 6.

and that as "the social relation is essentially a reciprocal relation, it gave a form of expression that has peculiar value."

This paper is an attempt to treat of the subjective
necessity for Social Settlements, to analyze the motives
which underlie a movement based not only upon conviction, but genuine emotion. Hull House of Chicago
is used as an illustration, but so far as the analysis is
faithful, it obtains wherever educated young people
are seeking an outlet for that sentiment of universal
brotherhood which the best spirit of our times is forcing from an emotion into a motive.

I have divided the motives which constitute the subjective pressure toward Social Settlements into three
great lines: the first contains the desire to make the
entire social organism democratic, to extend democracy beyond its political expression; the second is the
impulse to share the race life, and to bring as much
as possible of social energy and the accumulation of
civilization to those portions of the race which have
little; the third springs from a certain *renaissance* of
Christianity, a movement toward its early humanitarian aspects.

It is not difficult to see that although America is
pledged to the democratic ideal, the view of democracy has been partial, and that its best achievement
thus far has been pushed along the line of the franchise. Democracy has made little attempt to assert
itself in social affairs. We have refused to move beyond the position of its eighteenth-century leaders,
who believed that political equality alone would secure
all good to all men. We conscientiously followed the
gift of the ballot hard upon the gift of freedom to the

negro, but we are quite unmoved by the fact that he lives among us in a practical social ostracism. We hasten to give the franchise to the immigrant from a sense of justice, from a tradition that he ought to have it, while we dub him with epithets deriding his past life or present occupation, and feel no duty to invite him to our houses. . . .

. . . Our consciences are becoming tender in regard to the lack of democracy in social affairs. We are perhaps entering upon the second phase of democracy, as the French philosophers entered upon the first, somewhat bewildered by its logical conclusions. The social organism has broken down through large districts of our great cities. Many of the people living there are very poor, the majority of them without leisure or energy for anything but the gain of subsistence. They move often from one wretched lodging to another. They live for the moment side by side, many of them without knowledge of each other, without fellowship, without local tradition or public spirit, without social organization of any kind. Practically nothing is done to remedy this. The people who might do it, who have the social tact and training, the large houses, and the traditions and custom of hospitality, live in other parts of the city. The club-houses, libraries, galleries, and semi-public conveniences for social life are also blocks away. We find working-men organized into armies of producers because men of executive ability and business sagacity have found it to their interests thus to organize them. But these working-men are not organized socially; although living in crowded tenement-houses, they are living without a corresponding social contact. The chaos is as great as it would be were they working in huge factories without foreman or super-intendent. Their ideas and resources are cramped. The desire for higher social pleasure is extinct. They have no share in the traditions and social energy which make for progress. Too often their only place of meet-ing is a saloon, their only host a bartender; a local demagogue forms their public opinion. Men of abil-ity and refinement, of social power and university cul-tivation, stay away from them. Personally, I believe the men who lose most are those who thus stay away. But the paradox is here: when cultivated people do stay away from a certain portion of the population, when all social advantages are persistently withheld, it may be for years, the result itself is pointed at as a reason, is used as an argument, for the continued withholding. . . .

It is inevitable that those who feel most keenly this insincerity and partial living should be our young peo-ple, our so-called educated young people who accom-plish little toward the solution of this social problem, and who bear the brunt of being cultivated into un-nourished, over-sensitive lives. They have been shut off from the common labor by which they live and which is a great source of moral and physical health. They feel a fatal want of harmony between their theory and their lives, a lack of co-ordination between thought and action. I think it is hard for us to realize how seri-ously many of them are taking to the notion of human brotherhood, how eagerly they long to give tangible expression to the democratic ideal. These young men and women, longing to socialize their democracy, are animated by certain hopes.

These hopes may be loosely formulated thus: that

if in a democratic country nothing can be permanently achieved save through the masses of the people, it will be impossible to establish a higher political life than the people themselves crave; that it is difficult to see how the notion of a higher civic life can be fostered save through common intercourse; that the blessings which we associate with a life of refinement and cultivation can be made universal and must be made universal if they are to be permanent; that the good we secure for ourselves is precarious and uncertain, is floating in mid-air, until it is secured for all of us and incorporated into our common life.

These hopes are responsible for results in various directions, pre-eminently in the extension of educational advantages. We find that all educational matters are more democratic in their political than in their social aspects. The public schools in the poorest and most crowded wards of the city are inadequate to the number of children, and many of the teachers are ill-prepared and overworked; but in each ward there is an effort to secure public education. The school-house itself stands as a pledge that the city recognizes and endeavors to fulfil the duty of educating its children. But what becomes of these children when they are no longer in public schools? Many of them never come under the influence of a professional teacher nor a cultivated friend after they are twelve. Society at large does little for their intellectual development. The dream of transcendentalists that each New England village would be a university, that every child taken from the common school would be put into definite lines of study and mental development, had its unfulfilled beginning in the village lyceum and lecture courses, and has its feeble representative now in the multitude of clubs for study which are so sadly restricted to educators, to the leisure class, or only to the advanced and progressive wage-workers.

The University Extension movement — certainly when it is closely identified with Settlements — would not confine learning to those who already want it, or to those who, by making an effort, can gain it, or to those among whom professional educators are already at work, but would take it to the tailors of East London and the dock-laborers of the Thames. It requires tact and training, love of learning, and the conviction of the justice of its diffusion to give it to people whose intellectual faculties are untrained and disused. But men in England are found who do it successfully, and it is believed there are men and women in America who can do it. I also believe that the best work in University Extension can be done in Settlements, where the teaching will be further socialized, where the teacher will grapple his students, not only by formal lectures, but by every hook possible to the fuller intellectual life which he represents. This teaching requires distinct methods, for it is true of people who have been allowed to remain undeveloped and whose faculties are inert and sterile, that they cannot take their learning heavily. It has to be diffused in a social atmosphere. Information held in solution, a medium of fellowship and good-will can be assimilated by the dullest.

If education is, as Froebel defined it, "deliverance," deliverance of the forces of the body and mind, then the untrained must first be delivered from all constraint and rigidity before their faculties can be used. Possibly one of the most pitiful periods in the drama of the

much-praised young American who attempts to rise
in life is the time when his educational requirements
seem to have locked him up and made him rigid. He
fancies himself shut off from his uneducated family
and misunderstood by his friends. He is bowed down
by his mental accumulations and often gets no farther
than to carry them through life as a great burden. Not
once has he had a glimpse of the delights of knowledge.
Intellectual life requires for its expansion and manifestation the influence and assimilation of the interests
and affections of others. Mazzini, that greatest of all
democrats, who broke his heart over the condition of
the South European peasantry, said: "Education is not
merely a necessity of true life by which the individual
renews his vital force in the vital force of humanity;
it is a Holy Communion with generations dead and
living, by which he fecundates all his faculties. When
he is withheld from this Communion for generations,
as the Italian peasant has been, we point our finger
at him and say, 'He is like a beast of the field; he must
be controlled by force.'" Even to this it is sometimes
added that it is absurd to educate him, immoral to dis-
turb his content. We stupidly use again the effect as
an argument for a continuance of the cause. It is needless to say that a Settlement is a protest against a restricted view of education, and makes it possible for
every educated man or woman with a teaching faculty
to find out those who are ready to be taught. The social
and educational activities of a Settlement are but differing manifestations of the attempt to socialize democracy, as is the existence of the settlement itself.

I find it somewhat difficult to formulate the second
line of motives which I believe to constitute the trend

of the subjective pressure toward the Settlement. There
is something primordial about these motives, but I am
perhaps over-bold in designating them as a great desire
to share the race life. . . .

You may remember the forlorn feeling which occa-
sionally seizes you when you arrive early in the morning a stranger in a great city. The stream of laboring
people goes past you as you gaze through the plate-
glass window of your hotel. You see hard-working
men lifting great burdens; you hear the driving and
jostling of huge carts. Your heart sinks with a sudden
sense of futility. The door opens behind you and you
turn to the man who brings you in your breakfast with
a quick sense of human fellowship. You find yourself
praying that you may never lose your hold on it all
. . . . Literature is full of portrayals of these glimpses.
They come to shipwrecked men on rafts; they overcome
the differences of an incongruous multitude when in
the presence of a great danger or when moved by a
common enthusiasm. They are not, however, confined
to such moments, and if we were in the habit of telling
them to each other, the recital would be as long as the
tales of children are, when they sit down on the green
grass and confide to each other how many times they
have remembered that they lived once before. . . .

"There is nothing after disease, indigence, and a
sense of guilt so fatal to health and to life itself as the
want of a proper outlet for active faculties." I have seen
young girls suffer and grow sensibly lowered in vitality in the first years after they leave school. In our attempt then to give a girl pleasure and freedom from
care we succeed, for the most part, in making her piti-
fully miserable. She finds "life" so different from what

she expected it to be. She is besotted with innocent little ambitions, and does not understand this apparent
waste of herself, this elaborate preparation, if no work
is provided for her. There is a heritage of noble obligation which young people accept and long to perpetuate.
The desire for action, the wish to right wrong and alleviate suffering, haunts them daily. Society smiles at it
indulgently instead of making it of value to itself. . . .

We have in America a fast-growing number of cultivated young people who have no recognized outlet
for their active faculties. They hear constantly of the
great social mal-adjustment, but no way is provided for
them to change it, and their uselessness hangs about
them heavily. Huxley declares that the sense of uselessness is the severest shock which the human system can
sustain, and that, if persistently sustained, it results in
atrophy of function. These young people have had advantages of college, of European travel and economic
study, but they are sustaining this shock of inaction.
They have pet phrases, and they tell you that the things
that make us all alike are stronger than the things that
make us different. They say that all men are united
by needs and sympathies far more permanent and radical than anything that temporarily divides them and
sets them in opposition to each other. If they affect art,
they say that the decay in artistic expression is due to
the decay in ethics, that art when shut away from the
human interests and from the great mass of humanity
is self-destructive. They tell their elders with all the
bitterness of youth that if they expect success from
them in business, or politics, or in whatever lines their
ambition for them has run, they must let them consult
all of humanity; that they must let them find out what

the people want and how they want it. It is only the stronger young people, however, who formulate this. Many of them dissipate their energies in so-called enjoyment. Others, not content with that, go on studying and go back to college for their second degrees, not that they are especially fond of study, but because they want something definite to do, and their powers have been trained in the direction of mental accumulation. Many are buried beneath mere mental accumulation with lowered vitality and discontent. Walter Besant says they have had the vision that Peter had when he saw the great sheet let down from heaven, wherein was neither clean nor unclean. He calls it the sense of humanity. It is not philanthropy nor benevolence. It is a thing fuller and wider than either of these. This young life, so sincere in its emotion and good phrases and yet so undirected, seems to me as pitiful as the other great mass of destitute lives. One is supplementary to the other, and some method of communication can surely be devised. Mr. Barnett, who urged the first Settlement, — Toynbee Hall, in East London, — recognized this need of outlet for the young men of Oxford and Cambridge, and hoped that the Settlement would supply the communication. It is easy to see why the Settlement movement originated in England, where the years of education are more constrained and definite than they are here, where class distinctions are more rigid. The necessity of it was greater there, but we are fast feeling the pressure of the need and meeting the necessity for Settlements in America. Our young people feel nervously the need of putting theory into action, and respond quickly to the Settlement form of activity.

The third division of motives which I believe make toward the Settlement is the result of a certain *renaissance* going forward in Christianity. The impulse to share the lives of the poor, the desire to make social service, irrespective of propaganda, express the spirit of Christ, is as old as Christianity itself. . . .

That Christianity has to be revealed and embodied in the line of social progress is a corollary to the simple proposition that man's action is found in his social relationships in the way in which he connects with his fellows, that his motives for action are the zeal and affection with which he regards his fellows. By this simple process was created a deep enthusiasm for humanity, which regarded man as at once the organ and object of revelation; and by this process came about that wonderful fellowship, that true democracy of the early Church, that so captivates the imagination. The early Christians were pre-eminently non-resistant. They believed in love as a cosmic force. There was no iconoclasm during the minor peace of the Church. They did not yet denounce, nor tear down temples, nor preach the end of the world. They grew to a mighty number, but it never occurred to them, either in their weakness or their strength, to regard other men for an instant as their foes or as aliens. The spectacle of the Christians loving all men was the most astounding Rome had ever seen. They were eager to sacrifice themselves for the weak, for children and the aged. They identified themselves with slaves and did not avoid the plague. They longed to share the common lot that they might receive the constant revelation. It was a new treasure which the early Christians added to the sum of all treasures, a joy hitherto un-

known in the world — the joy of finding the Christ
which lieth in each man, but which no man can unfold save in fellowship. A happiness ranging from the
heroic to the pastoral enveloped them. They were to
possess a revelation as long as life had new meaning
to unfold, new action to propose.

I believe that there is a distinct turning among many
young men and women toward this simple acceptance
of Christ's message. They resent the assumption that
Christianity is a set of ideas which belong to the religious consciousness, whatever that may be, that it is
a thing to be proclaimed and instituted apart from the
social life of the community. They insist that it shall
seek a simple and natural expression in the social organism itself. The Settlement movement is only one
manifestation of that wider humanitarian movement
which throughout Christendom, but pre-eminently in
England, is endeavoring to embody itself, not in a sect,
but in society itself. Tolstoï has reminded us all very
forcibly of Christ's principle of non-resistance. His for-
mulation has been startling and his expression has de-
viated from the general movement, but there is little
doubt that he has many adherents, men and women
who are philosophically convinced of the futility of opposition, who believe that evil can be overcome only
with good and cannot be opposed. If love is the creative force of the universe, the principle which binds
men together, and by their interdependence on each
other makes them human, just so surely is anger and
the spirit of opposition the destructive principle of the
universe, that which tears down, thrusts men apart,
and makes them isolated and brutal.

I cannot, of course, speak for other Settlements, but

it would, I think, be unfair to Hull House not to emphasize the conviction with which the first residents went there, that it would simply be a foolish and an unwarrantable expenditure of force to oppose or to antagonize any individual or set of people in the neighborhood; that whatever of good the House had to offer should be put into positive terms; that its residents should live with opposition to no man, with recognition of the good in every man, even the meanest. I believe that this turning, this *renaissance* of the early Christian humanitarianism, is going on in America, in Chicago, if you please, without leaders who write or philosophize, without much speaking, but with a bent to express in social service, in terms of action, the spirit of Christ. Certain it is that spiritual force is found in the Settlement movement, and it is also true that this force must be evoked and must be called into play before the success of any Settlement is assured. There must be the overmastering belief that all that is noblest in life is common to men as men, in order to accentuate the likeness and ignore the differences which are found among the people whom the Settlement constantly brings into juxtaposition. . . .

If you have heard a thousand voices singing in the Hallelujah Chorus in Handel's "Messiah," you have found that the leading voices could still be distinguished, but that the differences of training and cultivation between them and the voices of the chorus were lost in the unity of purpose and the fact that they were all human voices lifted by a high motive. This is a weak illustration of what a Settlement attempts to do. It aims, in a measure, to lead whatever of social life its neighborhood may afford, to focus and give form to that life, to bring to bear upon it the results of cultivation and training; but it receives in exchange for the music of isolated voices the volume and strength of the chorus. . . .

The Settlement, then, is an experimental effort to aid in the solution of the social and industrial problems which are engendered by the modern conditions of life in a great city. It insists that these problems are not confined to any one portion of a city. It is an attempt to relieve, at the same time, the over-accumulation at one end of society and the destitution at the other; but it assumes that this over-accumulation and destitution is most sorely felt in the things that pertain to social and educational advantage. From its very nature it can stand for no political or social *propaganda*. It must, in a sense, give the warm welcome of an inn to all such *propaganda*, if perchance one of them be found an angel. The one thing to be dreaded in the Settlement is that it lose its flexibility, its power of quick adaptation, its readiness to change its methods as its environment may demand. It must be open to conviction and must have a deep and abiding sense of tolerance. It must be hospitable and ready for experiment. It should demand from its residents a scientific patience in the accumulation of facts and the steady holding of their sympathies as one of the best instruments for that accumulation. It must be grounded in a philosophy whose foundation is on the solidarity of the human race, a philosophy which will not waver when the race happens to be represented by a drunken woman or an idiot boy. Its residents must be emptied of all conceit of opinion and all self-assertion, and ready to arouse and interpret the public opinion of their neighborhood. They must be content to live quietly side by side with their neighbors until they grow into a sense of relationship and mutual interests. Their neighbors are held apart by differences of race and language which the residents can more easily overcome. They are bound to see the needs of their neighborhood as a whole, to furnish data for legislation, and use their influence to secure it. In short, residents are pledged to devote themselves to the duties of good citizenship and to the arousing of the social energies which too largely lie dormant in every neighborhood given over to industrialism. They are bound to regard the entire life of their city as organic, to make an effort to unify it, and to protest against its over-differentiation. . . .

. . . The Settlement movement is from its nature a provisional one. It is easy in writing a paper to make all philosophy point [to] one particular moral and all history adorn one particular tale; but I hope you forgive me for reminding you that the best speculative philosophy sets forth the solidarity of the human race; that the highest moralists have taught that without the advance and improvement of the whole no man can hope for any lasting improvement in his own moral or material individual condition. The subjective necessity for Social Settlements is identical with that necessity which urges us on toward social and individual salvation.

2

The College Woman
and the Family Claim

In this article Addams rather poignantly describes the difficulties she and other college women faced upon returning home after graduation. Although the piece details the particular situation of women college graduates of Addams's generation, it also deals with vocational conflicts that are perennial.

THE DAUGHTER AS A FAMILY POSSESSION.

It has always been difficult for the family to regard the daughter otherwise than as a family possession. From her babyhood she has been the charm and grace of the household, and it is hard to think of her as an integral part of the social order itself; to believe that she has duties outside of the family to the State and to society in the larger sense. This assumption in regard to the daughter that she was solely an inspiration and refinement to the family itself and its own immediate circle; that her delicacy and polish were but outward symbols of her father's protection and prosperity, worked very smoothly for the most part, so long as her education was in line with it. When there was absolutely no recognition of the entity of woman's life beyond the family, when the outside claims upon her were still wholly

SOURCE: *Commons* 3 (1898): 3–7. Excerpts of this article were reprinted in *Democracy and Social Ethics* (New York: Macmillan, 1902), chap. 3.

unrecognized, the situation was simple, and the finishing-school harmoniously and elegantly answered all requirements. She was fitted to grace the fireside and to add lustre to that social circle which her parents selected for her.

THE NEW INDIVIDUALITY
VERSUS THE OLD IDEAL.

This family assumption was notably broken into, however, when the daughter was sent to college. Her individuality was then recognized quite apart from family or society claims, and she received the sort of training which for many years has been deemed successful for highly developing a man's individuality and freeing his powers for independent action.

Perplexities often occur when the daughter returns home from college, owing to the fact that this recognition has been but partially accomplished. When she attempts to act upon the assumption of its accomplishment, she finds herself jarring upon ideals which are so entwined with filial piety, so rooted in the tenderest affections of which the human heart is capable, that both daughter and parents are shocked and startled when they discover what is happening, and they scarcely venture to formulate it because it implies the outrage of something sacred.

Wounded affection is sure to be the result when parental control and the family claim assert their authority in fields of effort which belong to adult judgment, and which pertain to activity outside of the family life. Probably the distinctively family tragedy, of

which we all catch glimpses now and then, is the assertion of this authority through all the entanglements
of wounded affection and misunderstanding. We see
both sides acting from conscientious motives and with
the tenderest affection, hiding their misery from each
other — a misery which is quite needless did they but
recognize the existence of more than one claim.

The ideal for the education of woman has doubtless
changed under the pressure of a new claim. The family
has responded to this claim to the extent of granting
an education in line with it, but they are still jealous
of it, and assert the family claim as over against it.

UNNECESSARY CONFLICT BETWEEN
THE SOCIAL AND THE FAMILY CLAIM.

The modern woman finds herself educated to recognize a stress of social obligation which her family did
not in the least anticipate when they sent her to college. In their view she has been educated that she
might well fulfill the duties of a daughter in a good
family and those belonging to a member of polite
society. She responds to these expectations, but she
finds herself, in addition, under an impulse to act her
part as a citizen of the world. She accepts her family
inheritance with loyalty and affection, but she has
entered into a wider inheritance as well. She has
strongly felt what the writer has ventured to call, for
lack of a better phrase, the human claim or the social
claim. The college woman submits her mind to the
latter for four years, only to find, after her return
from college, that the family claim is exclusively and

strenuously asserted, and that her attempts to fulfill the other are resented. The situation has all the discomfort of transition and compromise. The daughter finds a constant and totally unnecessary conflict between the social claim and the family claim. In most cases the social is repressed and gives way to the family claim, because the latter is concrete and definitely asserted, while the former is vague and unformulated. In such instances the girl quietly submits, but she feels in some way wronged whenever she allows her mind to dwell upon the situation. She either hides her hurt, and splendid reserves of enthusiasm and capacity go to waste, or her zeal and emotions are turned inward, and the result is an unhappy woman, whose vitality is consumed by vain regrets and desires.

A SHARE IN THE RACE LIFE COMPLETES THE FAMILY LIFE.

If the college woman who is freed from the necessity of self-support is not quietly reabsorbed into her family, she is even reproached for her discontent. She is told to be devoted to her family, inspiring and responsive to her social circle, and to give the rest of her time to further self-improvement and enjoyment. She expects to do this, and responds to these claims to the best of her ability—even heroically sometimes. But where is the larger life of which she has dreamed so long? that life of the race which surrounds and completes the individual and family life? She has been taught that it is her duty to share this life, and her highest privilege to extend it. This divergence between her self-centered existence and her best convictions becomes constantly more apparent. The situation is not even so simple as a conflict between her affections and her intellectual convictions, although even that is tumultuous enough; the emotional nature is divided against itself. The social claim is a demand upon the emotions as well as the intellect, and in ignoring that she not only represses her mental convictions, but lowers her springs of vitality. Her life is full of contradictions.

DOES MARRIAGE SATISFY THE UNIVERSAL CLAIM?

There is no doubt that the period when this tumult is greatest is the period between the daughter's graduation and her marriage, altho marriage by no means satisfies the universal claim. The young wife can offer us an excuse for a non-fulfillment of it that she gives much time to her household and to the care of her little children; but this excuse, like Ralph Touchet's weak lungs, alleviates her pangs of conscience, but does not satisfy her sense of unfulfilled obligation. The family claim in its highest form is being fulfilled, yet her full human claim is not thereby discharged. Many a young mother says to herself, "When my children are grown, then I shall give my time and ability to these outside things, which I really ought to do." There is no doubt that he who finds the family life in its sweetness and strength is he alone who fulfills the larger claim, just as truly as he who finds his individual life is he who first loses it.

NEED OF INITIATIVE TO ACTION.

The girl, however, cannot formulate this for herself. She looks out into the world longing that some demand be made upon her powers, for they are too untrained to furnish an initiative. When her health gives way under this strain, as it often does, her physician invariably advises a rest. But to be put to bed and fed on milk is not what she requires. What she needs is simple health-giving activity, which shall mean a response to all of the claims which she so keenly feels, and which shall involve the use of all her faculties.

It is quite true that the family often resents her first attempts to be part of a life quite outside their own, because the college woman frequently makes these first attempts most awkwardly; "visiting shiftless families; attending foolish meetings for the promotion of everything under the sun, and so on." Her faculties have not been trained in the line of action. She lacks the ability to apply her knowledge and theories, to Life itself and to its complicated situations. This is largely the fault of her training and of the one sidedness of educational methods. The colleges have long been full of the best ethical teaching insisting that the good of the whole must ultimately be the measure of effort, and that the individual can only secure his own rights as he labors to secure those of others. But while the college teaching has included an ever broadening range of obligation, and while it has insisted upon the recognition of the claims of human brotherhood, the college training has been singularly individualistic, it has fostered ambitions for personal distinction and has

trained the faculties almost exclusively in the direction of intellectual accumulation.

PRACTICAL DEFECT IN WOMAN'S EDUCATION.

Doubtless woman's education is at fault in that it has
failed to recognize certain needs and has failed to
cultivate and guide the great desires of which all generous young hearts are full. During the most forma-
tive years of life it gives the young girl no contact with
the feebleness of childhood, the pathos of suffering or
the needs of old age. It gathers together crude youth
in contact only with each other and with mature men
and women who are there for the purpose of their
mental direction. The tenderest promptings are bid-
den to bide their time. This could only be justifiable
if a definite outlet were provided when they leave college. Doubtless the need does not differ widely in
men and in women. But in the case of women, for
whom we may perhaps claim a more tender conscience,
those who are not absorbed in professional or business
life in the years immediately following college, are
brought baldly face to face with the fact that their
faculties have been stimulated in one direction and
trained in another. . . .

While the student is still in college the incongruity
between the ethical teaching and her training is largely
reconciled by dreams of future activity and it does not
bear upon her with unmitigated harshness. Because
of the ethics she has been taught but is not able to
formulate into action, — the same ethics which her

family much admire when actualized by a missionary or a philanthropist but which when undeveloped they insist are clashing with and disclaiming the family ties — we have all the elements of a tragedy. . . .

THE ATTITUDE OF MODERN PARENTS.

. . . Parents insist that the girl is carried away by a foolish enthusiasm, that she is in search of a career, that she is restless and does not know what she wants. They will give any reason, almost, rather than the recognition of a genuine and dignified claim. Possibly all this is due to the fact that for so many hundreds of years women have had no larger interests, no participation in the affairs lying quite outside of personal and family claims. Any attempt that the individual woman formerly made to subordinate or renounce the family claim was inevitably construed to mean, and often quite justly, that she was setting up her own will against that of her family for selfish ends. It was concluded that she could have no larger motive, and her attempt to break away was therefore selfish. That the family should consent to give her up at her marriage when she was enlarging the family tie by founding another family, was of course logical, or that they should permit and promote her going to college, traveling in Europe, or any other means of self-improvement, might merely mean the development and education of one of their own members; but an honest attempt to fulfill the universal claim was breaking away with every tradition. That the outward manifestation of the selfish attempt and of the larger attempt

are so similar, is of course an excuse for the family's
attitude. . . .

READJUSTMENT BETWEEN THE CLAIMS.

. . . As we have learned to adjust [the] two claims of
the personal and family, and to find an orderly development impossible without a recognition of both, so
perhaps we are called upon now to make a second adjustment, between the family and the universal, in
which neither shall lose and both be ennobled.

The family as well as the State we are all called upon
to maintain as the highest institutions which the race
has evolved for its safeguard and protection. But
merely to preserve these institutions is not enough.
There come periods of reconstruction, a task is laid
upon a passing generation, to enlarge the function and
carry forward the ideal of a long-established institution, that all coming generations may live in a larger
conception of it. There is no doubt that many women
consciously and unconsciously are struggling with this
task. The family, like every other element of human
life, is susceptible of progress, and from epoch to epoch
its tendencies and aspirations are enlarged, although
its duties can never be abrogated and its obligations
can never be canceled. It is impossible to bring about
the higher development by any self-assertion or breaking away of the individual will. The new growth in the
plant, swelling against the sheath which at the same
time imprisons and protects it, must still be the truest
type of progress. The family in its entirety must be
carried out into the larger life, it must lose none of its

affection but it must enlarge its affections and good-will until it embraces more than those held together by ties of consanguinity. To bring the notion of human brotherhood to bear upon active human life is not an easy undertaking. The harmonious, intelligent and consistent development of such a movement is as yet impossible; but let us at least cherish the manifestations of it even where they may seem ill judged. Let us avoid the error of considering those attempts unrighteous and something to be deplored, simply because our code of ethics has not yet been revised to fit this enlarged relationship.

3

A Function
of the Social Settlement

*Of central concern to Addams was the practical, applied value
of knowledge. In this discussion, she contrasts settlements' essentially pragmatic approach to knowledge with what she per-
ceived to be the more rigid, inert, "academic" approach of schools
and colleges.*

The word "settlement," which we have borrowed from
London, is apt to grate a little upon American ears.
It is not, after all, so long ago that Americans who settled were those who had adventured into a new country, where they were pioneers in the midst of difficult
surroundings. The word still implies migrating from
one condition of life to another totally unlike it, and
against this implication the resident of an American
settlement takes alarm.

We do not like to acknowledge that Americans are
divided into "two nations," as her prime minister once
admitted of England. We are not willing, openly and
professedly, to assume that American citizens are
broken up into classes, even if we make that assumption the preface to a plea that the superior class has
duties to the inferior. Our democracy is still our most
precious possession, and we do well to resent any in-

SOURCE: (*Annals of the American Academy of Political and Social
Science*) 13 (1899): 323–345. Later excerpted as "Social Settlement
and University Extension," *Review of Reviews* 20 (1899): 93.

roads upon it, even although they may be made in the name of philanthropy.

And yet because of this very democracy, superior privileges carry with them a certain sense of embarrassment, founded on the suspicion that intellectual and moral superiority too often rest upon economic props which are, after all, matters of accident, and that for an increasing number of young people the only possible way to be comfortable in the possession of those privileges, which result from educational advantages, is in an effort to make common that which was special and aristocratic. Added to this altruistic compunction one may easily discover a selfish suspicion that advantages thus held apart slowly crumble in their napkins, and are not worth having.

The American settlement, perhaps, has represented not so much a sense of duty of the privileged toward the unprivileged, of the "haves" to the "have nots," to borrow Canon Barnett's phrase, as a desire to equalize through social effort those results which superior opportunity may have given the possessor.

The settlement, however, certainly represents more than compunctions. Otherwise it would be but "the monastery of the nineteenth century," as it is indeed sometimes called, substituting the anodyne of work for that of contemplation, but still the old attempt to seek individual escape from the common misery through the solace of healing.

If this were the basis of the settlement, there would no longer be need of it when society had become reconstructed to the point of affording equal opportunity for all, and it would still be at the bottom a philanthropy, although expressed in social and democratic

terms. There is, however, a sterner and more enduring aspect of the settlement which this paper would
attempt to present.

It is frequently stated that the most pressing problem of modern life is that of a reconstruction and a
reorganization of the knowledge which we possess; that
we are at last struggling to realize in terms of life all
that has been discovered and absorbed, to make it over
into healthy and direct expressions of free living. Dr.
John Dewey, of the University of Chicago, has written: "Knowledge is no longer its own justification, the
interest in it has at last transferred itself from accumulation and verification to its application to life." And
he adds: "When a theory of knowledge forgets that its
value rests in solving the problem out of which it has
arisen, that of securing a method of action, knowledge
begins to cumber the ground. It is a luxury, and becomes a social nuisance and disturber."

We may quote further from Professor James, of
Harvard University, who recently said in an address
before the Philosophical Union of the University of
California: "Beliefs, in short, are really rules of action,
and the whole function of thinking is but one step in
the production of habits of action," or "the ultimate
test for us of what a truth means is indeed the conduct it dictates or inspires."

Having thus the support of two philosophers, let us
assume that the dominating interest in knowledge has
become its use, the conditions under which, and ways
in which it may be most effectively employed in human conduct; and that at last certain people have consciously formed themselves into groups for the express
purpose of effective application. These groups which

are called settlements have naturally sought the spots where the dearth of this applied knowledge was most obvious, the depressed quarters of great cities. They gravitate to these spots, not with the object of finding clinical material, not to found "sociological laboratories," not, indeed, with the analytical motive at all, but rather in a reaction from that motive, with a desire to use synthetically and directly whatever knowledge they, as a group, may possess, to test its validity and to discover the conditions under which this knowledge may be employed.

That, just as groups of men, for hundreds of years, have organized themselves into colleges, for the purpose of handing on and disseminating knowledge already accumulated, and as other groups have been organized into seminars and universities, for the purpose of research and the extension of the bounds of knowledge, so at last groups have been consciously formed for the purpose of the application of knowledge to life. This third attempt also would claim for itself the enthusiasm and advantage of collective living. It has come to be a group of people who share their methods, and who mean to make experience continuous beyond the individual. It may be urged that this function of application has always been undertaken by individuals and unconscious groups. This is doubtless true, just as much classic learning has always been disseminated outside of the colleges, and just as some of the most notable discoveries of pure science have been made outside of the universities. Still both these institutions do in the main accomplish the bulk of the disseminating, and the discovering; and it is upon the same basis that the third group may establish its value.

The ideal and developed settlement would attempt
to test the value of human knowledge by action, and
realization, quite as the complete and ideal university
would concern itself with the discovery of knowledge
in all branches. The settlement stands for application
as opposed to research; for emotion as opposed to abstraction, for universal interest as opposed to specialization. This certainly claims too much, absurdly too
much, for a settlement, in the light of its achievements,
but perhaps not in the light of its possibilities.

This, then, will be my definition of the settlement:
that it is an attempt to express the meaning of life in
terms of life itself, in forms of activity. There is no
doubt that the deed often reveals when the idea does
not, just as art makes us understand and feel what
might be incomprehensible and inexpressible in the
form of an argument. And as the artist tests the success of his art when the recipient feels that he knew
the thing before, but had not been able to express it,
so the settlement, when it attempts to reveal and apply
knowledge, deems its results practicable, when it has
made knowledge available which before was abstract,
when through use, it has made common that knowledge which was partial before, because it could only
be apprehended by the intellect.

The chief characteristic of art lies in freeing the individual from a sense of separation and isolation in
his emotional experience, and has usually been accomplished through painting, writing and singing; but this
does not make it in the least impossible that it is now
being tried, self-consciously and most bunglingly we
will all admit, in terms of life itself.

A settlement brings to its aid all possible methods

to reveal and make common its conception of life. All those arts and devices which express kindly relation from man to man, from charitable effort to the most specialized social intercourse, are constantly tried. There is the historic statement, the literary presentation, the fellowship which comes when great questions are studied with the hope of modifying actual conditions, the putting forward of the essential that the trivial may appear unimportant, as it is, the attempt to select the more typical and enduring forms of social life, and to eliminate, as far as possible, the irrelevant things which crowd into actual living. There are so-called art exhibits, concerts, dramatic representations, every possible device to make operative on the life around it, the conception of life which the settlement group holds. The demonstration is made not by reason, but by life itself. There must, of course, be a certain talent for conduct and unremitting care lest there grow to be a divergence between theory and living, for however embarrassing this divergence may prove in other situations, in a settlement the artist throws away his tools as soon as this thing happens. He is constantly transmitting by means of his human activity, his notion of life to others. He hopes to produce a sense of infection which may ultimately result in identity of interest.

Merely to produce a sense of infection would be art, but to carry with it a consciousness of participation and responsibility would be the moralizing and application of art. We may illustrate this with that form of art which is most general and prevalent among us, the art of novel writing. No one who has ever read Zangwill's "Children of the Ghetto" can afterwards walk

through the Jewish quarter of any great city without
a quickening of the blood as he passes. He must feel
a momentary touch of the poetry and fidelity which
are fostered there, the power of an elaborate ceremo-
nial and carefully preserved customs. Let us add to
this revelation of literature a personal acquaintance
with a young man whose affection and loyalty, whose
tenderest human ties and domestic training are pulling
one way against the taste and desires of a personality
which constantly draws him into pursuits and interests
outside of the family life. We may see, day after day,
his attempts to attend ceremonies for which he no
longer cares, his efforts to interest his father in other
questions, and to transfer his religious zeal to social
problems. We have added to Zangwill's art by our personal acquaintance, a dramatic force which even he
could not portray. We may easily know a daughter
who might earn much more money as a stenographer,
could she work from Monday morning to Saturday
night, but who quietly and docilely makes neckties for
low wages because she can thus abstain from work Sat-
urdays, to please her father. She goes without the
clothes she otherwise might have, she identifies herself
with girls whom she does not care for, in order to avoid
the break which would be so desperate. Without Zangwill's illumination we would have to accumulate much
more experience, but it is no compliment to the artist,
if, having read him, we feel no desire for experience
itself.

   After all, the only world we know is that of Appreciation, but we grow more and more discontented
with a mere intellectual apprehension, and wish to
move forward from a limited and therefore obscure

understanding of life to a larger and more embracing one, not only with our minds, but with all our powers of life. Our craving for art is a desire to appreciate emotionally, our craving for life is a desire to move forward organically.

I know little Italian boys who joyfully drop their English the moment they are outside the school-room door; and others of them who are teaching the entire family and forming a connection between them and the outside world, interpreting political speeches and newspapers and eagerly transforming Italian customs into American ones. One watches the individual boy with great interest, to see whether he will faithfully make himself a transmitter and helper, or whether he will be stupidly pleased with his achievements, and consider his examinations the aim of his life. I sometimes find myself nervously watching a young man or woman in a university in much the same way, and applying essentially the same test. I wonder whether his knowledge will in the end exercise supreme sway over him, so that he will come to consider it "a self-sufficing purveyor of reality," and care for nothing further, whether he will become, in the end, "school bound" with his faculties well trained for acquisition, but quite useless in other directions. To test a student's knowledge of Italian history by a series of examinations is possible; to test his genuine interest in that great boot thrust into the Mediterranean is to know whether or not he conquers a comparatively easy language, whether he traces in the large Italian colony of his city the hero-worship and higher aims evoked by Garibaldi as they are gradually seized upon by the ward politician and converted to ignoble ends; whether

he feels a certain shame that, although Mazzini dedicated to the working men of Italy his highest ethical
and philosophical appeal so that a desire for a republic
had much to do with their coming to America, no
great teacher of ethics or politics has ever devoted
himself to the Italians in America. Just as we do not
know a fact until we can play with it, so we do not
possess knowledge until we have an impulse to bring
it into use; not the didactic impulse, not the propa-
gandist impulse, but that which would throw into the
stream of common human experience one bit of important or historic knowledge, however small, which
before belonged to a few.

The phrase "applied knowledge" or science has so
long been used in connection with polytechnic schools
that it may be well to explain that I am using it in a
broader sense. These schools have applied science
primarily for professional ends. They are not so commercial, but they may easily become quite as specialized in their departments as the chemical laboratories
attached to certain large manufacturing concerns. In
the early days of Johns Hopkins University, one of the
men in the biological department invented a contriv-
ance which produced a very great improvement in the
oyster raft at that time in use in the Chesapeake Bay.
For months afterward, in all the commencement ora-
tions and other occasions when "prominent citizens"
were invited to speak, this oyster raft was held up as
the great contribution of the University to the commercial interest of the city, and as a justification of the
University's existence, much to the mortification of the
poor inventor. This, also, is an excellent example of
what I do not mean.

The application which I have in mind is one which cannot be measured by its money-making value. I have in mind an application to a given neighborhood of the solace of literature, of the uplift of the imagination, and of the historic consciousness which gives its possessor a sense of connection with the men of the past who have thought and acted, an application of the stern mandates of science, not only to the conditions of sewers and the care of alleys, but to the methods of life and thought; the application of the metaphysic not only to the speculations of the philosopher, but to the events of the passing moment; the application of the moral code to the material life, the transforming of the economic relation into an ethical relation until the sense that religion itself embraces all relations, including the ungodly industrial relation, has become common property.

An ideal settlement would have no more regard for the "commercial" than would the most scientific of German seminars. The word application must be taken quite aside from its commercial or professional sense.

In this business of application, however, a settlement finds itself tending not only to make common those good things which before were partial and remote, but it finds itself challenging and testing by standards of moral democracy those things which it before regarded as good, if they could but be universal, and it sometimes finds that the so-called good things will not endure this test of being universalized. This may be illustrated by various good things. We may take first the so-called fine arts.

Let us consider the experience of a resident of a settlement who cares a great deal for that aspect and history of life, which has been portrayed in the fine arts. For years she has had classes studying through photographs and lectures the marbles of Greece, the paintings, the renaissance of Italy and the Gothic architecture of mediaeval Europe. She has brought into the lives of scores of people a quality of enjoyment, a revelation of experience which they never knew before. Some of them buy photographs to hang in their own houses, a public school art society is started, schoolroom walls are tinted and hung with copies of the best masters; so that in the end hundreds of people have grown familiar with the names of the artists, and with conceptions of life which were hidden from them before. Some of these young women were they students of a fresh-water college could successfully pass an examination in the "History of Art." The studio of Hull House is well filled with young men and women who successfully copy casts and paint accurately what they see around them, and several of them have been admitted to the Chicago Art Institute upon competitive scholarships. Now, the first of these achievements would certainly satisfy the average college teacher whose business it is faithfully to transmit the accumulations of knowledge upon a given subject, and, of course, if possible, to add to the sum total of that knowledge in the matter of arrangement or discovery. The second achievement would certainly satisfy the ordinary philanthropic intent, which is to give to others the good which it possesses. But a settlement would have little vitality if it were satisfied with either of these achievements, and would at once limit its scope to that of the school on the one hand, or that of philanthropy on the other. And a settlement is neither a school nor a philanthropy, nor yet a philanthropic school or a scholarly philanthropy.

This may indeed bring us quite naturally to the attitude of the settlement toward the organized education with which it is brought in contact, the two forms of organization being naturally the public school and university extension lectures.

The resident finds the use of the public school constantly limited because it occupies such an isolated place in the community. The school board and the teachers have insensibly assumed that they have to do exclusively with children, or a few adult evening classes, only in certain settled directions. The newly arrived South Italian peasants who come to the night schools are thoroughly ill-adjusted to all their surroundings. To change suddenly from picking olives to sewer extension is certainly a bewildering experience. They have not yet obtained control of their powers for the performance of even the humblest social service, and have no chance to realize within themselves the social relation of that service which they are performing. Feeling this vaguely perhaps, but very strongly as only a dull peasant mind can feel, they go to the night schools in search of education. They are taught to read and write concerning small natural objects, on the assumption that the undeveloped intellect works best with insects and tiny animals, and they patiently accept this uninteresting information because they expect "education" to be dull and hard. Never for an instant are their own problems of living in the midst of unfamiliar surroundings even touched upon. There seems to be a belief among educators that it is not possible for the mass of mankind to have experiences which are of themselves worth anything, and that accordingly, if a neighborhood is to receive valuable ideas at all, they must be brought in from the outside, and almost exclusively in the form of books. Such scepticism regarding the possibilities of human nature as has often been pointed out results in equipping even the youngest children with the tools of reading and writing, but gives them no real participation in the industrial and social life with which they come in contact.

The residents in a settlement know that for most of their small neighbors life will be spent in handling material things either in manufacturing or commercial processes, and yet little is done to unfold the fascinating history of industrial evolution or to illuminate for them the materials among which they will live. The settlement sees boys constantly leave school to enter the factory at fourteen or fifteen without either of the requirements involved in a social life, on the one hand "without a sense of the resources already accumulated," and on the other "without the individual ability to respond to those resources."

If it is one function of a settlement to hold a clue as to what to select and what to eliminate in the business of living, it would bring the same charge of overwrought detail against the university extension lectures. A course of lectures in astronomy, illustrated by "stereopticon slides," will attract a large audience the first week who hope to hear of the wonders of the heavens, and the relation of our earth thereto, but instead of that they are treated to spectrum analyses of star dust, or the latest theories concerning the milky way. The habit of research and the desire to say the latest word upon any subject overcoming any sympathetic understanding of his audience which the lecturer might otherwise develop.

The teachers in the night schools near Hull House struggle with Greeks and Armenians, with Bohemians and Italians, and many another nationality. I once suggested to a professor of anthropology in a neighboring university that he deliver a lecture to these bewildered teachers upon simple race characteristics and, if possible, give them some interest in their pupils, and some other attitude than that all persons who do not speak English are ignorant. The professor kindly consented to do this, but when the time came frankly acknowledged that he could not do it — that he had no information available for such a talk. I was disappointed, of course, and a little chagrined when, during the winter, three of his pupils came to me at different times, anxiously inquiring if I could not put them on the track of people who had six toes, or whose relatives had been possessed of six toes. It was inevitable that the old charge should occur to me, that the best trained scientists are inclined to give themselves over to an idle thirst for knowledge which lacks any relation to human life, and leave to the charlatans the task of teaching those things which deeply concern the welfare of mankind.

Tolstoy points out that the mass of men get their intellectual food from the abortive outcasts of science, who provide millions of books, pictures and shows, not to instruct and guide, but for the sake of their own profit and gain, while the real student too often stays in a laboratory, occupied in a mysterious activity called science. He does not even know what is required by the workingmen. He has quite forgotten their mode of life, their views of things and their language. Tolstoy claims that the student has lost sight of the fact that it is his duty, not to study and depict, but to serve. This is asking a great deal from one man, or even from one institution. It may be necessary that the university be supplemented by the settlement, or something answering thereto; but let the settlement people recognize the value of their own calling, and see to it that the university does not swallow the settlement, and turn it into one more laboratory: another place in which to analyze and depict, to observe and record. A settlement which performs but this function is merely an imitative and unendowed university, as a settlement which gives all its energies to classes and lectures and athletics is merely an imitative college. We ourselves may have given over attending classes and may be bored by lectures, but to still insist that working people shall have them is to take the priggish attitude we sometimes allow ourselves toward children, when we hold up rigid moral standards to them, although permitting ourselves a greater latitude. If without really testing the value of mental pabulum, we may assume it is nutritious and good for working people, because some one once assumed that it was good for us, we throw away the prerogative of a settlement, and fall into the rigidity of the conventional teacher.

So far as my experience goes a settlement finds itself curiously more companionable with the state and national bureaus in their efforts in collecting information and analyzing the situation, than it does with university efforts. This may possibly be traced to the fact that the data is accumulated by the bureaus on the assumption that it will finally become the basis for legislation, and is thus in the line of applicability. The settlements from the first have done more or less work under the direction of the bureaus. The head of a federal department quite recently begged a settlement to transform into readable matter a certain mass of material which had been carefully collected into tables and statistics. He hoped to make a connection between the information concerning diet and sanitary conditions, and the tenement house people who sadly needed this information. The head of the bureau said quite simply that he hoped that the settlements could accomplish this, not realizing that to put information into readable form is not nearly enough. It is to confuse a simple statement of knowledge with its application.

Permit me to illustrate from a group of Italian women who bring their underdeveloped children several times a week to Hull House for sanitary treatment, under the direction of a physician. It has been possible to teach some of these women to feed their children oatmeal instead of tea-soaked bread, but it has been done, not by statement at all but by a series of gay little Sunday morning breakfasts given to a group of them in the Hull House nursery. A nutritious diet was thus substituted for an inferior one by a social method. At the same time it was found that certain of the women hung bags of salt about their children's necks, to keep off the evil eye, which was supposed to give the children crooked legs at first, and in the end to cause them to waste away. The salt bags gradually disappeared under the influence of baths and cod liver oil. In short, rachitis was skillfully arrested, and without mention that disease was caused not by evil eye but by lack of cleanliness and nutrition, and without passing through the intermediate belief that disease was sent by Providence, the women form a little centre for the intelligent care of children, which is making itself felt in the Italian colony. Knowledge was applied in both cases, but scarcely as the statistician would have applied it.

We recall that the first colleges of the Anglo-Saxon race were established to educate religious teachers. For a long time it was considered the mission of the educated to prepare the mass of the people for the life beyond the grave. Knowledge dealt largely in theology, but it was ultimately to be applied, and the test of the successful graduate, after all, was not his learning, but his power to save souls. As the college changed from teaching theology to teaching secular knowledge the test of its success should have shifted from the power to save men's souls to the power to adjust them in healthful relations to nature and their fellow men. But the college failed to do this, and made the test of its success the mere collecting and disseminating of knowledge, elevating the means into an end and falling in love with its own achievement. The application of secular knowledge need be no more commercial and so-called practical than was the minister's when he applied his theology to the delicate problems of the human soul. This attempt at application on the part of the settlements may be, in fact, an apprehension of the situation.

It would be a curious result if this word "applied science," which the scholar has always been afraid of, lest it lead him into commercial influences, should have in it the salt of saving power, to rescue scholarship from the function of accumulating and transmitting to the higher and freer one of directing human life.

Recognizing the full risk of making an absurd, and as yet totally unsubstantiated claim, I would still express the belief that the settlement has made a genuine contribution in this direction by its effort to apply knowledge to life, to express life itself in terms of life.

In line with this conception are the efforts the settlement makes to mitigate the harshness of industry by this legal enactment. The residents are actuated, not by a vague desire to do good which may distinguish the philanthropist, nor by that thirst for data and analysis of the situation which so often distinguishes the "sociologist," but by the more intimate and human desire that the working man, quite aside from the question of the unemployed or the minimum wage, shall have secured to him powers of life and enjoyment, after he has painstakingly earned his subsistence; that he shall have an opportunity to develop those higher moral and intellectual qualities upon which depend the free aspects and values of living. Thus a settlement finds itself more and more working toward legal enactment, not only on behalf of working people, and not only in cooperation with them, but with every member of the community who is susceptible to the moral appeal. Labor legislation has always been difficult in America, largely owing to our optimism, and the comparative ease of passing from class to class. The sweater's victim, who hopes soon to be a contractor himself, will not take an interest in the law which may momentarily protect him but which may later operate against him. A man who is a bricklayer ambitious to become a master builder is not too eager that building regulations be made more stringent. In order to get a law, even to protect a small class of citizens, an appeal has to be made to the moral sense of the entire community, for one is barred from the very nature of the case from making a class appeal. Hundreds of girls are constantly impaired in health and vitality by long hours of factory work, yet each one of these girls is so confident of marrying out of her trade, — each one regards her factory work as so provisional, that it is almost impossible to secure among them a concerted movement for improvement. To make a sensational appeal on their behalf or on behalf of the sweater's victims is undemocratic and often accentuates the consciousness of class difference. When the newspapers tell us of the horrors of the sweat shop, painting one shop with the various shades of blackness, found only in a dozen, until no human being however wretched could possibly work in such a shop, it becomes all the more difficult to set before the public mind what a reasonable workshop demands. Orderliness and cleanliness do not seem necessary to the mind sated with the horrors of contagious diseases. To impress upon such a mind that sweaters' employees live out but half the days of even the short life of the working man cannot arouse it to concern. When, in order to excite pity for one family a newspaper will degrade all humanity in the minds of the benevolent of the community, so that the statement that the poor lose fifty per cent of their children, does not seem startling if they die quietly in their beds and are not frozen and starved, is to increase the gulf beyond what actually exists. The sensational writer of short stories, who recklessly overstates and holds the exceptional as the habitual, does much to destroy the conception of human life, which experience has been slowly building up in the minds of the community. A reckless appeal to primitive pity may change conditions of a given case, but it sacrifices too much for the result.

A settlement in its attempt to apply the larger knowledge of life to industrial problems makes its appeal upon the assumption that the industrial problem is a social one, and the effort of a settlement in securing labor legislation is valuable largely in proportion as it can make both the working men and the rest of the community conscious of solidarity, and insists upon similarities rather than differences. A settlement constantly endeavors to make its neighborhood realize that it belongs to the city as a whole, and can only improve as the city improves. We, at Hull House, have undertaken to pave the streets of our ward only to find that we must agitate for an ordinance, that repaving shall be done from a general fund before we can hope to have our streets properly paved. We have attempted to compel by law, that the manufacturer provide proper work rooms for his sweater's victims, and were surprised to find ourselves holding a mass meeting in order to urge a federal measure upon Congress.

One of the residents at Hull House for three years faithfully inspected the alleys of our ward, but all her faithful service was set at naught because civil service has been but a farce in Chicago and to insist upon its administration, and the abolition of the contract system is the shortest method of cleaning the alleys.

The settlement was startled during October and November of last year by the occurrence of seven murders within a radius of ten blocks from Hull House, in a neighborhood of which we had always boasted that it was not criminal. A little investigation of details and motives, the accident of a personal acquaintance with two of the criminals, made it not in the least difficult to trace the murders back to the influence of the late war between Spain and the United States. The predatory instinct is not far back of most of us. Simple people who read of carnage and bloodshed easily receive a suggestion. Habits of self-control which have been but slowly and imperfectly acquired quickly break down. Some psychologists intimate that action germinates not only in the habitual thought, but may be traced to the selection of the subject upon which the attention is fixed and that it is by this decision of what shall hold the attention that the trend of action is determined. The newspapers, the posters, the street conversation for weeks had to do with war and threatening of war.

The little children in the street played at war day after day, although they did not play they were freeing Cubans, but on the contrary that they were killing Spaniards. For years the settlement had held that the life of each little child should be regarded as valuable, that the humane instinct should keep in abeyance any tendency to cruelty, that law and order should be observed, not only in letter, but in spirit, and it suddenly finds that a national event has thrown back all this effort.

There is no doubt that we grow more or less accustomed to faults and follies which we constantly see, and that a resident leaving one quarter of the city for another does get a fresher point of view. She comes in to an industrial neighborhood to find that the workingmen living there see those of their own numbers who have gradually yielded to a love of drink and have become drunkards, with a certain amount of indifference and leniency of judgment. Many of these wretched men have been kindly good natured fellows, and possessed of weak wills rather than vicious ones. The resident is shocked by this leniency, but in course of time she finds herself viewing business circles from a new point of view. A business man constantly sees men around him who have gradually yielded to a love of money until many of them have become perjurers, in order to avoid the payment of full taxes; some of them have lent themselves to debauching city councils and state legislatures in order to protect vested interests by "necessary legislation;" yet a business man finds himself tending to judge such conduct leniently because it is a temptation which he can understand, one to which he himself has more or less yielded at least by connivance, if not by participation. To habitually drink too much alcohol and neglect one's wife and children, or to annually perjure one's soul and neglect one's duty to the state, are not really so unlike in motive and consequence, to anyone who looks at them freely and from an equidistant standpoint.

Our attention has so long been called to the sins of the appetite and to the neglect of family obligations, that we fail to see these other equally great sins of cupidity and failure to respond to the social duty. To fail to see social dereliction in one class and point out moral failure in the drunkard shows a singular lack of understanding of the ethical problems which are now pressing upon us. Books have been written on the poverty and wretchedness which are the result of alcoholism, and it has indeed been overworked rather than underworked as a cause of social deterioration. Social disorders arising from conscienceless citizenship have yet to be made clear.

There are doubtless two dangers to which the settlement is easily susceptible. The first is the danger that it shall approach too nearly the spirit of the mission which, as Canon Barnett has recently pointed out, in the Nineteenth Century Review, will always exist, will always be needed, but which from its very nature can not be a settlement. Those who join it believe in some doctrines or methods which they wish to extend, it may be those of church, of socialists, or teetotallers, of political party; but followers are enlisted and organized and a vast amount of machinery created for a given aim. They will always be able to tell how many they have "reached," and how many believe as they do. As Canon Barnett says there are moments when definiteness of doctrine and the measuring of men's motives must seem the most essential thing and at such times the settlement must appear ineffective; but so far as a settlement group is committed to one philosophy which it cares for above the meanings which life may teach, so far as definiteness precludes perception, so far as their minds are not free to rise and fall with their neighbor's minds, which are occupied with hundreds of cares and hopes, so far a settlement has failed.

The second danger is the tendency to lay stress upon what we might call "geographical salvation." All over the world from Russia west to Japan people are moving from country to town, with the conviction that they are finding more fullness of life. An advance guard may be said to be moving back from the town to the country, from the sprinkling of the very rich to the little colonies, found in England and America, who are protesting against the industrial system by getting out of it so far as possible. But within the limits of the city itself, also can be found this belief in geographical salvation. When a given neighborhood becomes shabby, or filled with foreigners, whose habits are unlike those of their neighbors, the best people in the neighborhood begin to move out, taking with them their initiative and natural leadership, as their parents had previously taken it from their native villages. A settlement deliberately selects such a neighborhood, and moves into it, but must not lay too much stress upon that fact in and of itself. Its social relations are successful as it touches to life the dreary and isolated, and brings them into a fuller participation of the common inheritance. Its teaching is successful as it makes easy and available that which was difficult and remote. Its most valuable function as yet, lies along the line of interpretation and synthesis.

4

Educational Methods

In this forceful condemnation of narrowly commercial school curricula, Addams calls for educational practices that will help to alleviate the deadening routines of industrial work. She argues that for a truly democratic society to exist, occupational status cannot be determinative of social status, and hence, that the first purpose of education must be to give all people the interests and the sense of dignity and civic worth that will enable them to transcend the limits imposed by their daily pursuits. Here, as in many of her other writings, Addams presents educational reform as a necessary step toward more fundamental political reform.

As democracy modifies our conception of life, it constantly raises the value and function of each member of the community, however humble he may be. We have come to believe that the most "brutish man" has a value in our common life, a function to perform which can be fulfilled by no one else. We are gradually requiring of the educator that he shall free the powers of each man and connect him with the rest of life. We ask this not merely because it is the man's right to be thus connected, but because we have become convinced that the social order cannot afford to get along without his special contribution. Just as we have come to resent all hindrances which keep us from untram-

SOURCE: *Democracy and Social Ethics* (New York: Macmillan, 1902), chap. 6.

melled comradeship with our fellows, and as we throw down unnatural divisions, not in the spirit of the eighteenth-century reformers, but in the spirit of those to whom social equality has become a necessity for further social development, so we are impatient to use the dynamic power residing in the mass of men, and demand that the educator free that power. We believe that man's moral idealism is the constructive force of progress, as it has always been; but because every human being is a creative agent and a possible generator of fine enthusiasm, we are sceptical of the moral idealism of the few and demand the education of the many, that there may be greater freedom, strength, and subtilty of intercourse and hence an increase of dynamic power. We are not content to include all men in our hopes, but have become conscious that all men are hoping and are part of the same movement of which we are a part.

Many people impelled by these ideas have become impatient with the slow recognition on the part of the educators of their manifest obligation to prepare and nourish the child and the citizen for social relations. The educators should certainly conserve the learning and training necessary for the successful individual and family life, but should add to that a preparation for the enlarged social efforts which our increasing democracy requires. The democratic ideal demands of the school that it shall give the child's own experience a social value; that it shall teach him to direct his own activities and adjust them to those of other people. We are not willing that thousands of industrial workers shall put all of their activity and toil into services from which the community as a whole reaps the benefit, while their mental conceptions and code of morals are narrow and untouched by any uplift which the consciousness of social value might give them.

We are impatient with the schools which lay all stress on reading and writing, suspecting them to rest upon the assumption that the ordinary experience of life is worth little, and that all knowledge and interest must be brought to the children through the medium of books. Such an assumption fails to give the child any clew to the life about him, or any power to usefully or intelligently connect himself with it. . . .

If we admit that in education it is necessary to begin with the experiences which the child already has and to use his spontaneous and social activity, then the city streets begin this education for him in a more natural way than does the school. The South Italian peasant comes from a life of picking olives and oranges, and he easily sends his children out to pick up coal from railroad tracks, or wood from buildings which have been burned down. Unfortunately, this process leads by easy transition to petty thieving. It is easy to go from the coal on the railroad track to the coal and wood which stand before a dealer's shop; from the potatoes which have rolled from a rumbling wagon to the vegetables displayed by the grocer. This is apt to be the record of the boy who responds constantly to the stimulus and temptations of the street, although in the beginning his search for bits of food and fuel was prompted by the best of motives.

The school has to compete with a great deal from the outside in addition to the distractions of the neighborhood. Nothing is more fascinating than that mysterious "down town," whither the boy longs to go to sell papers and black boots, to attend theatres, and, if possible, to stay all night on the pretence of waiting for the early edition of the great dailies. If a boy is once thoroughly caught in these excitements, nothing can save him from over-stimulation and consequent debility and worthlessness; he arrives at maturity with no habits of regular work and with a distaste for its dulness.

On the other hand, there are hundreds of boys of various nationalities who conscientiously remain in school and fulfil all the requirements of the early grades, and at the age of fourteen are found in factories, painstakingly performing their work year after year. These later are the men who form the mass of the population in every industrial neighborhood of every large city; but they carry on the industrial processes year after year without in the least knowing what it is all about. The one fixed habit which the boy carries away with him from the school to the factory is the feeling that his work is merely provisional. In school the next grade was continually held before him as an object of attainment, and it resulted in the conviction that the sole object of present effort is to get ready for something else. This tentative attitude takes the last bit of social stimulus out of his factory work; he pursues it merely as a necessity, and his very mental attitude destroys his chance for a realization of its social value. As the boy in school contracted the habit of doing his work in certain hours and taking his pleasure in certain other hours, so in the factory he earns his money by ten hours of dull work and spends it in three hours of lurid and unprofitable pleasure in the evening. Both in the school and in the factory, in proportion as his work grows dull and monotonous, his recreation must become more exciting and stimulating. The hopelessness of adding evening classes and social entertainments as a mere frill to a day filled with monotonous and deadening drudgery constantly becomes more apparent to those who are endeavoring to bring a fuller life to the industrial members of the community, and who are looking forward to a time when work shall cease to be senseless drudgery with no self-expression on the part of the worker. It sometimes seems that the public schools should contribute much more than they do to the consummation of this time. If the army of school children who enter the factories every year possessed thoroughly vitalized faculties, they might do much to lighten this incubus of dull factory work which presses so heavily upon so large a number of our fellow-citizens. Has our commercialism been so strong that our schools have become insensibly commercialized, whereas we supposed that our industrial life was receiving the broadening and illuminating effects of the schools? The training of these children, so far as it has been vocational at all, has been in the direction of clerical work. It is possible that the business men, whom we in America so tremendously admire, have really been dictating the curriculum of our public schools, in spite of the conventions of educators and the suggestions of university professors. The business man, of course, has not said, "I will have the public schools train office boys and clerks so that I may have them easily and cheaply," but he has sometimes said, "Teach the children to write legibly and to figure accurately and quickly; to acquire habits of punctuality and order; to be prompt to obey;

and you will fit them to make their way in the world as I have made mine." Has the workingman been silent as to what he desires for his children, and allowed the business man to decide for him there, as he has allowed the politician to manage his municipal affairs, or has the workingman so far shared our universal optimism that he has really believed that his children would never need to go into industrial life at all, but that all of his sons would become bankers and merchants?

Certain it is that no sufficient study has been made of the child who enters into industrial life early and stays there permanently, to give him some offset to its monotony and dulness, some historic significance of the part he is taking in the life of the community.

It is at last on behalf of the average workingmen that our increasing democracy impels us to make a new demand upon the educator. As the political expression of democracy has claimed for the workingman the free right of citizenship, so a code of social ethics is now insisting that he shall be a conscious member of society, having some notion of his social and industrial value.

The early ideal of a city that it was a market-place in which to exchange produce, and a mere trading-post for merchants, apparently still survives in our minds and is constantly reflected in our schools. We have either failed to realize that cities have become great centres of production and manufacture in which a huge population is engaged, or we have lacked sufficient presence of mind to adjust ourselves to the change. We admire much more the men who accumulate riches, and who gather to themselves the results of industry, than the men who actually carry forward industrial processes; and, as has been pointed out, our schools still prepare children almost exclusively for commercial and professional life.

Quite as the country boy dreams of leaving the farm for life in town and begins early to imitate the travelling salesman in dress and manner, so the school boy within the town hopes to be an office boy, and later a clerk or salesman, and looks upon work in the factory as the occupation of ignorant and unsuccessful men. The schools do so little really to interest the child in the life of production, or to excite his ambition in the line of industrial occupation, that the ideal of life, almost from the very beginning, becomes not an absorbing interest in one's work and a consciousness of its value and social relation, but a desire for money with which unmeaning purchases may be made and an unmeaning social standing obtained.

The son of a workingman who is successful in commercial life, impresses his family and neighbors quite as does the prominent city man when he comes back to dazzle his native town. The children of the working people learn many useful things in the public schools, but the commercial arithmetic, and many other studies, are founded on the tacit assumption that a boy rises in life by getting away from manual labor, — that every promising boy goes into business or a profession. The children destined for factory life are furnished with what would be most useful under other conditions, quite as the prosperous farmer's wife buys a folding-bed for her huge four-cornered "spare room," because her sister, who has married a city man, is obliged to have a folding-bed in the cramped limits of her flat.

Partly because so little is done for him educationally, and partly because he must live narrowly and dress meanly, the life of the average laborer tends to become flat and monotonous, with nothing in his work to feed his mind or hold his interest. Theoretically, we would all admit that the man at the bottom, who performs the meanest and humblest work, so long as the work is necessary, performs a useful function; but we do not live up to our theories, and in addition to his hard and uninteresting work he is covered with a sort of contempt, and unless he falls into illness or trouble, he receives little sympathy or attention. Certainly no serious effort is made to give him a participation in the social and industrial life with which he comes in contact, nor any insight and inspiration regarding it.

Apparently we have not yet recovered manual labor from the deep distrust which centuries of slavery and the feudal system have cast upon it. To get away from menial work, to do obviously little with one's hands, is still the desirable status. This may readily be seen all along the line. A workingman's family will make every effort and sacrifice that the brightest daughter be sent to the high school and through the normal school, quite as much because a teacher in the family raises the general social standing and sense of family consequence, as that the returns are superior to factory or even office work. "Teacher" in the vocabulary of many children is a synonym for women-folk gentry, and the name is indiscriminately applied to women of certain dress and manner. The same desire for social advancement is expressed by the purchasing of a piano, or the fact that the son is an office boy, and not a factory hand. The overcrowding of the professions by poorly equipped men arises from much the same source, and from the conviction that, "an education" is wasted if a boy goes into a factory or shop. . . .

Quite in line with this commercial ideal are the night schools and institutions of learning most accessible to working people. First among them is the business college which teaches largely the mechanism of type-writing and book-keeping, and lays all stress upon commerce and methods of distribution. Commodities are treated as exports and imports, or solely in regard to their commercial value, and not, of course, in relation to their historic development or the manufacturing processes to which they have been subjected. These schools do not in the least minister to the needs of the actual factory employee, who is in the shop and not in the office. We assume that all men are searching for "puddings and power," to use Carlyle's phrase, and furnish only the schools which help them to those ends.

The business college man, or even the man who goes through an academic course in order to prepare for a profession, comes to look on learning too much as an investment from which he will later reap the benefits in earning money. He does not connect learning with industrial pursuits, nor does he in the least lighten or illuminate those pursuits for those of his friends who have not risen in life. "It is as though nets were laid at the entrance to education, in which those who by some means or other escape from the masses bowed down by labor, are inevitably caught and held from substantial service to their fellows." The academic teaching which is accessible to workingmen through University Extension lectures and classes at settlements, is usually bookish and remote, and concerning subjects completely divorced from their actual experiences. The men come to think of learning as something to be added to the end of a hard day's work, and to be gained at the cost of toilsome mental exertion. There are, of course, exceptions, but many men who persist in attending classes and lectures year after year find themselves possessed of a mass of inert knowledge which nothing in their experience fuses into availability or realization.

Among the many disappointments which the settlement experiment has brought to its promoters, perhaps none is keener than the fact that they have as yet failed to work out methods of education, specialized and adapted to the needs of adult working people in contra-distinction to those employed in schools and colleges, or those used in teaching children. There are many excellent reasons and explanations for this failure. In the first place, the residents themselves are for the most part imbued with academic methods and ideals, which it is most difficult to modify. To quote from a late settlement report, "The most vaunted educational work in settlements amounts often to the stimulation mentally of a select few who are, in a sense, of the academic type of mind, and who easily and quickly respond to the academic methods employed." These classes may be valuable, but they leave quite untouched the great mass of the factory population, the ordinary workingman of the ordinary workingman's street, whose attitude is best described as that of "acquiescence," who lives through the aimless passage of the years without incentive "to imagine, to design, or to aspire." These men are totally untouched by all the educational and philanthropic machinery which is designed for the young and the helpless who live on the same streets with them. They do not often drink to excess, they regularly give all their wages to their wives, they have a vague pride in their superior children; but they grow prematurely old and stiff in all their muscles, and become more and more taciturn, their entire energies consumed in "holding a job."

Various attempts have been made to break through the inadequate educational facilities supplied by commercialism and scholarship, both of which have followed their own ideals and have failed to look at the situation as it actually presents itself. The most noteworthy attempt has been the movement toward industrial education, the agitation for which has been ably seconded by manufacturers of a practical type, who have from time to time founded and endowed technical schools, designed for workingmen's sons. The early schools of this type inevitably reflected the ideal of the self-made man. They succeeded in transferring a few skilled workers into the upper class of trained engineers, and a few less skilled workers into the class of trained mechanics, but did not aim to educate the many who are doomed to the unskilled work which the permanent specialization of the division of labor demands.

The Peter Coopers and other good men honestly believed that if intelligence could be added to industry, each workingman who faithfully attended these schools could walk into increased skill and wages, and in time even become an employer himself. Such schools are useful beyond doubt; but so far as educating workingmen is concerned or in any measure satisfying the democratic ideal, they plainly beg the question.

Almost every large city has two or three polytechnic

institutions founded by rich men, anxious to help "poor boys." These have been captured by conventional educators for the purpose of fitting young men for the colleges and universities. They have compromised by merely adding to the usual academic course manual work, applied mathematics, mechanical drawing and engineering. Two schools in Chicago, plainly founded for the sons of workingmen, afford an illustration of this tendency and result. On the other hand, so far as schools of this type have been captured by commercialism, they turn out trained engineers, professional chemists, and electricians. They are polytechnics of a high order, but do not even pretend to admit the workingman with his meagre intellectual equipment. They graduate machine builders, but not educated machine tenders. Even the textile schools are largely seized by young men who expect to be superintendents of factories, designers, or manufacturers themselves, and the textile worker who actually "holds the thread" is seldom seen in them; indeed, in one of the largest schools women are not allowed, in spite of the fact that spinning and weaving have traditionally been woman's work, and that thousands of women are at present employed in the textile mills.

It is much easier to go over the old paths of education with "manual training" thrown in, as it were; it is much simpler to appeal to the old ambitions of "getting on in life," or of "preparing for a profession," or "for a commercial career," than to work out new methods on democratic lines. These schools gradually drop back into the conventional courses, modified in some slight degree, while the adaptation to workingmen's needs is never made, nor, indeed, vigorously attempted. In the meantime, the manufacturers continually protest that engineers, especially trained for devising machines, are not satisfactory. Three generations of workers have invented, but we are told that invention no longer goes on in the workshop, even when it is artifically stimulated by the offer of prizes, and that the inventions of the last quarter of the nineteenth century have by no means fulfilled the promise of the earlier three-quarters.

Every foreman in a large factory has had experience with two classes of men: first with those who become rigid and tolerate no change in their work, partly because they make more money "working by the piece," when they stick to that work which they have learned to do rapidly, and partly because the entire muscular and nervous system has become by daily use adapted to particular motions and resents change. Secondly, there are the men who float in and out of the factory, in a constantly changing stream. They "quit work" for the slightest reason or none at all, and never become skilled at anything. Some of them are men of low intelligence, but many of them are merely too nervous and restless, too impatient, too easily "driven to drink," to be of any use in a modern factory. They are the men for whom the demanded adaptation is impossible.

The individual from whom the industrial order demands ever larger drafts of time and energy, should be nourished and enriched from social sources, in proportion as he is drained. He, more than other men, needs the conception of historic continuity in order to reveal to him the purpose and utility of his work, and he can only be stimulated and dignified as he obtains a conception of his proper relation to society. Scholar-

ship is evidently unable to do this for him; for, unfortunately, the same tendency to division of labor has
also produced over-specialization in scholarship, with
the sad result that when the scholar attempts to minister to a worker, he gives him the result of more
specialization rather than an offset from it. He cannot bring healing and solace because he himself is suffering from the same disease. There is indeed a de-
plorable lack of perception and adaptation on the part
of educators all along the line.

It will certainly be embarrassing to have our age
written down triumphant in the matter of inventions,
in that our factories were filled with intricate machines,
the result of advancing mathematical and mechanical
knowledge in relation to manufacturing processes, but
defeated in that it lost its head over the achievement
and forgot the men. The accusation would stand, that
the age failed to perform a like service in the extension
of history and art to the factory employees who ran
the machines; that the machine tenders, heavy and almost dehumanized by monotonous toil, walked about
in the same streets with us, and sat in the same cars;
but that we were absolutely indifferent and made no
genuine effort to supply to them the artist's perception or student's insight, which alone could fuse them
into social consciousness. It would further stand that
the scholars among us continued with yet more research, that the educators were concerned only with
the young and the promising, and the philanthropists
with the criminals and helpless.

There is a pitiful failure to recognize the situation
in which the majority of working people are placed,
a tendency to ignore their real experiences and needs,

and, most stupid of all, we leave quite untouched affections and memories which would afford a tremendous dynamic if they were utilized.

We constantly hear it said in educational circles,
that a child learns only by "doing," and that education must proceed "through the eyes and hands to the
brain"; and yet for the vast number of people all
around us who do not need to have activities artificially
provided, and who use their hands and eyes all the
time, we do not seem able to reverse the process. We
quote the dictum, "What is learned in the schoolroom
must be applied in the workshop," and yet the skill and
handicraft constantly used in the workshop have no
relevance or meaning given to them by the school; and
when we do try to help the workingman in an educational way, we completely ignore his everyday occupation. Yet the task is merely one of adaptation. It is to
take actual conditions and to make them the basis for
a large and generous method of education, to perform
a difficult idealization doubtless, but not an impossible
one.

We apparently believe that the workingman has no
chance to realize life through his vocation. We easily
recognize the historic association in regard to ancient
buildings. We say that "generation after generation
have stamped their mark upon them, have recorded
their thoughts in them, until they have become the
property of all." And yet this is even more true of the
instruments of labor, which have constantly been held
in human hands. A machine really represents the
"seasoned life of man" preserved and treasured up
within itself, quite as much as an ancient building
does. At present, workmen are brought in contact with

the machinery with which they work as abruptly as if the present set of industrial implements had been newly created. They handle the machinery day by day, without any notion of its gradual evolution and growth. Few of the men who perform the mechanical work in the great factories have any comprehension of the fact that the inventions upon which the factory depends, the instruments which they use, have been slowly worked out, each generation using the gifts of the last and transmitting the inheritance until it has become a social possession. This can only be understood by a man who has obtained some idea of social progress. We are still childishly pleased when we see the further subdivision of labor going on, because the quantity of the output is increased thereby, and we apparently are unable to take our attention away from the product long enough to really focus it upon the producer. Theoretically, "the division of labor" makes men more interdependent and human by drawing them together into a unity of purpose. "If a number of people decide to build a road, and one digs, and one brings stones, and another breaks them, they are quite inevitably united by their interest in the road. But this naturally presupposes that they know where the road is going to, that they have some curiosity and interest about it, and perhaps a chance to travel upon it." If the division of labor robs them of interest in any part of it, the mere mechanical fact of interdependence amounts to nothing.

The man in the factory, as well as the man with the hoe, has a grievance beyond being overworked and disinherited, in that he does not know what it is all about. We may well regret the passing of the time when the variety of work performed in the unspecialized workshop naturally stimulated the intelligence of the workingmen and brought them into contact both with the raw material and the finished product. But the problem of education, as any advanced educator will tell us, is to supply the essentials of experience by a short cut, as it were. If the shop constantly tends to make the workman a specialist, then the problem of the educator in regard to him is quite clear: it is to give him what may be an offset from the over-specialization of his daily work, to supply him with general information and to insist that he shall be a cultivated member of society with a consciousness of his industrial and social value.

As sad a sight as an old hand-loom worker in a factory attempting to make his clumsy machine compete with the flying shuttles about him, is a workingman equipped with knowledge so meagre that he can get no meaning into his life nor sequence between his acts and the far-off results.

Manufacturers, as a whole, however, when they attempt educational institutions in connection with their factories, are prone to follow conventional lines, and to exhibit the weakness of imitation. We find, indeed, that the middle-class educator constantly makes the mistakes of the middle-class moralist when he attempts to aid working people. The latter has constantly and traditionally urged upon the workingman the specialized virtues of thrift, industry, and sobriety — all virtues pertaining to the individual. When each man had his own shop, it was perhaps wise to lay almost exclusive stress upon the industrial virtues of diligence and thrift; but as industry has become more highly

organized, life becomes incredibly complex and interdependent. If a workingman is to have a conception
of his value at all, he must see industry in its unity and
entirety; he must have a conception that will include
not only himself and his immediate family and community, but the industrial organization as a whole. It
is doubtless true that dexterity of hand becomes less
and less imperative as the invention of machinery and
subdivision of labor proceeds; but it becomes all the
more necessary, if the workman is to save his life at
all, that he should get a sense of his individual relation
to the system. Feeding a machine with a material of
which he has no knowledge, producing a product,
totally unrelated to the rest of his life, without in the
least knowing what becomes of it, or its connection with
the community, is, of course, unquestionably deadening to his intellectual and moral life. To make the
moral connection it would be necessary to give him
a social consciousness of the value of his work, and at
least a sense of participation and a certain joy in its
ultimate use; to make the intellectual connection it
would be essential to create in him some historic conception of the development of industry and the relation of his individual work to it.

Workingmen themselves have made attempts in
both directions, which it would be well for moralists
and educators to study. It is a striking fact that when
workingmen formulate their own moral code, and try
to inspire and encourage each other, it is always a large
and general doctrine which they preach. They were
the first class of men to organize an international
association, and the constant talk at a modern labor
meeting is of solidarity and of the identity of the in-

terests of workingmen the world over. It is difficult to
secure a successful organization of men into the
simplest trades organization without an appeal to the
most abstract principles of justice and brotherhood.
As they have formulated their own morals by laying
the greatest stress upon the largest morality, so if they
could found their own schools, it is doubtful whether
they would be of the mechanic institute type. Courses
of study arranged by a group of workingmen are most
naïve in their breadth and generality. They will select
the history of the world in preference to that of any
period or nation. The "wonders of science" or "the story
of evolution" will attract workingmen to a lecture when
zoölogy or chemistry will drive them away. The
"outlines of literature" or "the best in literature" will
draw an audience when a lecturer in English poetry
will be solitary. This results partly from a wholesome
desire to have general knowledge before special knowledge, and is partly a rebound from the specialization
of labor to which the workingman is subjected. When
he is free from work and can direct his own mind, he
tends to roam, to dwell upon large themes. Much the
same tendency is found in programmes of study arranged by Woman's Clubs in country places. The untrained mind, wearied with meaningless detail, when
it gets an opportunity to make its demand heard, asks
for general philosophy and background.

In a certain sense commercialism itself, at least in
its larger aspect, tends to educate the workingman
better than organized education does. Its interests are
certainly world-wide and democratic, while it is absolutely undiscriminating as to country and creed,
coming into contact with all climes and races. If this

aspect of commercialism were utilized, it would in a measure counterbalance the tendency which results from the subdivision of labor.

The most noteworthy attempt to utilize this democracy of commerce in relation to manufacturing is found at Dayton, Ohio, in the yearly gatherings held in a large factory there. Once a year the entire force is gathered together to hear the returns of the business, not so much in respect to the profits, as in regard to its extension. At these meetings, the travelling salesmen from various parts of the world — from Constantinople, from Berlin, from Rome, from Hong Kong — report upon the sales they have made, and the methods of advertisement and promotion adapted to the various countries.

Stereopticon lectures are given upon each new country as soon as it has been successfully invaded by the product of the factory. The foremen in the various departments of the factory give accounts of the increased efficiency and the larger output over former years. Any man who has made an invention in connection with the machinery of the factory, at this time publicly receives a prize, and suggestions are approved that tend to increase the comfort and social facilities of the employees. At least for the moment there is a complete esprit de corps, and the youngest and least skilled employee sees himself in connection with the interests of the firm, and the spread of an invention. It is a crude example of what might be done in the way of giving a large framework of meaning to factory labor, and of putting it into a sentient background, at least on the commercial side.

It is easy to indict the educator, to say that he has

gotten entangled in his own material, and has fallen
a victim to his own methods; but granting this, what
has the artist done about it — he who is supposed to
have a more intimate insight into the needs of his contemporaries, and to minister to them as none other
can?

It is quite true that a few writers are insisting that
the growing desire for labor, on the part of many people of leisure, has its counterpart in the increasing
desire for general knowledge on the part of many
laborers. They point to the fact that the same duality
of conscience which seems to stifle the noblest effort
in the individual because his intellectual conception
and his achievement are so difficult to bring together,
is found on a large scale in society itself, when we have
the separation of the people who think from those who
work. And yet, since Ruskin ceased, no one has really
formulated this in a convincing form. And even Ruskin's famous dictum, that labor without art brutalizes,
has always been interpreted as if art could only be a
sense of beauty or joy in one's own work, and not a
sense of companionship with all other workers. The
situation demands the consciousness of participation
and well-being which comes to the individual when
he is able to see himself "in connection and cooperation with the whole"; it needs the solace of collective
art inherent in collective labor.

As the poet bathes the outer world for us in the hues
of human feeling, so the workman needs some one to
bathe his surroundings with a human significance —
some one who shall teach him to find that which will
give a potency to his life. His education, however simple, should tend to make him widely at home in the

world, and to give him a sense of simplicity and peace
in the midst of the triviality and noise to which he is
constantly subjected. He, like other men, can learn
to be content to see but a part, although it must be
a part of something.

It is because of a lack of democracy that we do not
really incorporate him in the hopes and advantages
of society, and give him the place which is his by
simple right. We have learned to say that the good
must be extended to all of society before it can be held
secure by any one person or any one class; but we have
not yet learned to add to that statement, that unless
all men and all classes contribute to a good, we cannot
even be sure that it is worth having. In spite of many
attempts we do not really act upon either statement.

5

The Humanizing Tendency
of Industrial Education

Briefly, but with evocative detail, Addams writes here again of "educational methods." She focuses on exchanges of knowledge, skill, and experience between people of different nationalities and generations. Education as mutual efforts to share unusual talents and traditions was the basis for community as Addams understood it.

A glimpse of the Hull-House shops on a busy evening incites the imagination as to what the ideal public school might offer during the long winter nights, if it became really a "center" for its neighborhood. We could imagine the business man teaching the immigrant his much needed English and arithmetic and receiving in return lessons in the handling of tools and materials so that they should assume in his mind a totally different significance from that the factory gives them, as the resulting product would possess for him the delicacy and charm which the self-expression of the workers always implies. Even the cant phrase of the "dignity of labor" might receive a new meaning. The kitchen, which every ideal school possesses, could give opportunity for Italian women to teach their neighbors how to cook the delicious macaroni, such a different thing from the semi-elastic product which Americans honor with that name. The peasant soups, the national

SOURCE: *Chautauquan* 34 (1904): 266–272.

dishes which old European travelers boast about, could with a little care be discovered and revived. To learn to speak English would be a comparatively easy thing for an Italian woman while she was handling kitchen utensils and was in the midst of familiar experiences — it would be a very different matter from learning it in the cramped, unnatural position which sitting at a child's school desk implies, using a book with a sense of bewilderment.

Their desire to learn to make "American clothes for the children" could easily be gratified by kindly American women who realize how slow the Italian women are to adapt their children's clothing to this severe climate and how bitterly they suffer illness and loss because of this lack of adaptation, but in return the American woman would receive demonstration of the early textile methods, little exhibits of petticoats and kerchiefs such as would make her own clothing look cheap and uninteresting. She would receive a lesson in "the estimating of wealth in terms of life" which would be worth ten chapters in Ruskin or as many lectures on "the Consumers' League."

More than that, the American woman would have issued forth from her own experience into the understanding of some one who spoke a different language, whose life had been spent in widely divergent activities. She would have been able to do this through that quickened historic perception and that enlarged power of human intercourse which is supposed to divide the cultivated person from the limited person, the cosmopolitan from the provincial. It would really be a large return for her simple service to the Italian woman.

If we imagine these activities going on in the public

school of the future, it would, of course, be equipped with swimming baths where the famous divers of the Bay of Naples could well give lessons to the rest, as indeed the workmen often do now in the school gymnasiums. It is not difficult to see that the peasant, the newly arrived emigrant, would have an opportunity to "teach" his American neighbor which the present evening school, supplied almost solely with the apparatus for reading and writing, utterly denies to him. The average American firmly believes that in order to know European life he must cross over to Europe, and he remains perfectly oblivious to the fact that at least in its essential industries, in its historic implication and charm, it has already crossed over to us.

The Labor Museum at Hull-House has been able to put into historic sequence and order ten methods of spinning, from the Syrian to the Norwegian, and almost as many methods of weaving. These have all been collected from the resources of the neighborhood itself, not that spinning and weaving may be taught, but that their development may be demonstrated by reproduction of the actual processes, so that the many young people who work in the tailoring trades, who make neckties and who knit underwear, may have some idea of the material they are handling and of its connection with the long effort of their parents and grandparents.

So long as so-called cultured Americans judge "foreigners" from the most superficial standpoint and without any attempt to know them from the historically industrial standpoint, we can scarcely be surprised that the children of the foreigners quickly grow ashamed of them because they do not speak English nor wear de-

partment store clothes. That narrow standard of judgment is responsible for much loneliness, bitterness of
spirit and strained affection, and digs ever deeper that
gulf between father and sons which might be avoided
did we but realize the humanizing power, the healing
which lies in genuine industrial education.

6

Child Labor
Legislation — A Requisite
for Industrial Efficiency

In 1904 Addams helped establish the National Child Labor Committee to lobby for compulsory schooling and uniform national child labor laws. This is a speech given to that committee. It illustrates her deep respect for play as a form of education as well as her belief that schooling is "primary" to the subsequent opportunities for education that are offered largely, though not exclusively, at places of work. Given this view, Addams argues that it is both inhumane and inefficient to allow children to enter the labor force at young ages. Such practices, she insists, stunt the development of the young and, by robbing them of appropriate educational experiences in childhood, which may diminish their intelligence and imagination as adults, harm the nation.

We continually assert that we are living in an industrial age and on many occasions we openly boast of our industrial achievements; it is, for instance, almost impossible to make an acceptable Fourth of July oration without impressive mention of the railroads and telegraph lines "which bind together a mighty conti-

SOURCE: National Child Labor Committee, *Proceedings of the First Annual Conference*, New York City, February 14–16, 1905, pp. 128–136. Reprinted in *Annals of the American Academy of Political and Social Science* 25 (1905): 542–550.

nent." Although in our moments of expansiveness we so fully admit this successful industrialism, at other times we seem to be ashamed of it and continually insist that we must find our culture, our religion and our education quite outside of it, as if the inner world developed in complete independence of the outer. This may be one reason that our culture, our religion and our education so often seem weak and feeble compared to our industrialism. We fail to realize that because we are living in an industrial age we must find our culture through that industry, and that to seek culture in some other age that is not our own is to wear a borrowed and ill-fitting garment; that if we fail to apply our religion to the industrial situation and refuse to be guided by it through the problems which current industrialism develops, that it perforce becomes meaningless and remote, and that even more is this true in regard to education. A school which fails to give outlet and direction to the growing intelligence of the child "to widen and organize his experience with reference to the world in which he lives" merely dresses his mind in antiquated precepts and gives him no clue to the life which he must lead. It was formerly assumed that a child went to school unwillingly, and that he there entered into an unending struggle with his teacher, who was often justified in the use of coercion. The new pedagogy . . . holds that it is a child's instinct and pleasure to exercise all his faculties and to make discoveries in the world around him, that it is the chief business of the teacher merely to direct his activity and to feed his insatiable curiosity. In order to accomplish this he is forced to relate the child to the surroundings in which he lives, and the most advanced schools are using modern industry for this purpose.

Educators have ceased to mourn the changed industrial conditions in which children were taught agricul-
tural and industrial arts by natural co-operation with
their parents, and they are endeavoring to supply this
disadvantage by manual arts in the school, by courses
in industrial history, and by miniature reproductions
of industrial processes, thus constantly coming into
better relations with the present factory system.

The advocates for child labor legislation . . . are
most heartily in sympathy with this new standpoint,
and in several notable instances the advanced educator
is he who is most conspicuously striving for adequate
legal protection for the child. The members of this
conference are in no sense those who advocate a life
of idleness or of meaningless activity for the growing
child, nor do they believe in a spurious or "leisure class"
culture. On the contrary I hope to be able to show that
because we recognize the significance and power of
contemporary industrialism . . . we hold it an obligation to protect children from premature participation
in its mighty operations, not only that they may secure
the training and fibre which will later make that participation effective, but that their minds may finally
take possession of the machines which they will guide
and feed.

There has been for many years an increasing criticism of the modern factory system, both from the point
of view of the worker and from the point of view of
the product itself. It has been said many times that we
cannot secure good workmanship nor turn out a satisfactory product unless men and women have some sort
of interest in their work, and some way of expressing
that interest in relation to it. The system which makes

no demand upon originality, upon invention, upon self-direction, works automatically, as it were, towards an unintelligent producer and towards an uninteresting product. This was at first said only by such artists and social reformers as Morris and Ruskin, but it is being gradually admitted by men of affairs and may at last incorporate itself into actual factory management, in which case the factory itself will favor child labor legislation or any other measure which increases the free and full development of the individual, because he thereby becomes a more valuable producer. We may gradually discover that in the interests of this industrial society of ours it becomes a distinct loss to put large numbers of producers prematurely at work, not only because the community inevitably loses their mature working power, but also because their "free labor quality," which is so valuable, is permanently destroyed. Exercise of the instinct of workmanship not only affords great satisfaction to the producer, but also to the consumer who is possessed of any critical faculty.

We are told that the German products hold a foremost place in the markets of the world because of Germany's fine educational system, which includes training in trade schools for so many young men, and that there is at the present moment a strong party in Germany opposing militarism, not from the "peace society" point of view, but because it withdraws all of the young men from industrial life for the best part of three years, during which time their activity is merely disciplinary, with no relation to the industrial life of the nation. This anti-military party insists that the loss of the three years is serious, and the nation cannot successfully hold its advanced place if it must compete with those nations

who do not thus withdraw their youth from continuous training at the period of their greatest docility and
aptitude.

. . . It would be easy to produce other illustrations
to demonstrate that in the leading industrial countries
a belief is slowly developing that the workman himself
is the chief asset, and that the intelligent interest of
skilled men, that power of self-direction and co-operation which is only possible among the free born and
educated, is exactly the only thing which will hold out
in the markets of the world. As the foremen of factories
will testify again and again, factory discipline is valuable only up to a certain point, after which they must
depend upon something else if they would achieve the
best results.

The smallest child I ever saw at work was in a southern mill, — a little girl of five walked up and down her
short lane in a spindle room. The product the mill was
turning out was cotton sheeting of the coarsest sort,
which was said to be designed for use in the Chinese
army. Quite naturally a child of five, holding her snuff
stick against her first "milk-teeth" and tying threads
with her clumsy baby hands, could not contribute to
a product demanding care and skill, and a mill which
used up the labor power of its community in such reckless fashion could never hope to compete with the product turned out in another community in which a large
share of the mechanics had been carefully educated
in the public school and in which the municipality itself sustained a textile school.

Monopoly of the raw material and newly-opened
markets are certainly valuable factors in a nation's
industrial prosperity, but while we spend blood and

treasure to protect the one and to secure the other, we wantonly destroy the most valuable factor of all, which is intelligent labor.

We have made public education our great concern in America and perhaps the public school system is our most distinctive achievement, but there is a certain lack of consistency in the relation of the state to the child after he leaves the public school. At a great expense the state has provided school buildings and equipment, and yet other buildings in which to prepare professional teachers. It has spared no pains to make the system complete, and yet as rapidly as the children leave the school room the state seems to lose all interest and responsibility in their welfare, and has, until quite recently, turned them over to the employer, with no restrictions as to the number of hours he shall permit them to work, nor as to the sort of employment which he shall give them. The Webbs long ago used in illustration of this contradictory attitude of the state the story of an employer who might ask the state to equip his factory with machinery of recent invention that he might use it for his own profit and with but the incidental benefit to the community; at the end of a few years finding it worn out, he would again apply for a new equipment of a later device and value, throwing the old back upon the state which had previously given it to him. The Webbs insist that this is analogous to the employer asking the state for children, who have been educated in the public schools, demanding that they be especially drilled in habits of obedience and promptness and in those practical studies which make them the most useful to him; he puts them to work, and if they are worn out at the termination of a few years by labor beyond their strength, the state will have to care for some of them in its hospitals and poorhouses, but it takes them back without a word of protest against the employer who demands a fresh lot, educated in accordance with his requirements, which he may again overwork without any interference from the state. At no point does the community say we have allowed you to profit by the labor of these children whom we have educated at great cost, and we demand that they do not work so many hours that they shall be exhausted, nor shall they be allowed to undertake the sort of labor which is beyond their strength, nor shall they spend their time at work which is absolutely devoid of educational value. The preliminary education which they have received in school is but one step in the process of making them valuable and normal citizens, and we cannot afford to have that intention thwarted, even though the community as well as yourself may profit by the business activity which your factory affords. Such a position seems perfectly reasonable, and yet the same citizens who willingly pay taxes to support an elaborate public school system strenuously oppose the most moderate attempts to guard the children from needless and useless exploitation after they have left school and have entered industry. . . .

Uniform compulsory education laws in connection with uniform child labor legislation are the important factors in securing educated producers for the nation, but there is another side to the benefits of child labor legislation represented by the *time element*, the leisure which is secured to the child for the pursuit of his own affairs, quite aside from the opportunity afforded him to attend school. Helplessness in childhood, the scientists tell us, is the guarantee of adult intellect, but they also assert that play in youth is the guarantee of adult culture. It is the most valuable instrument the race possesses to keep life from becoming mechanical. The child who cannot live life is prone to dramatize it, and the very process is a constant compromise between imitation and imagination as the overmastering impulse itself which drives him to incessant play is both reminiscent and anticipatory. In proportion as the child in later life is to be subjected to a mechanical and one-sided activity and as a highly-subdivided labor is to be demanded from him, it is therefore most important that he should have his full period of childhood and youth for this play expression, that he may cultivate within himself the root of that culture which can alone give his later activity a meaning, and this is true whether or not we accept the theory that the aesthetic feelings originate from the play impulse with its corollary — that the constant experimentation found in the commonest plays are to be looked upon as "the principal source of all kinds of art." In this moment, when individual forces are concentrated and unified as never before, unusual care must be taken to secure to the children their normal play period, that the art instinct may have some chance and that the producer himself may have enough coherence of character to avoid becoming a mere cog in the vast industrial machine.

Quite aside also from the individual development and from the fact that play in which the power of choice is constantly presented and constructive imagination required is the best corrective of the future disciplinary life of the factory, there is another reason why the children who are to become producers under the present system should be given their full child-life period.

The entire population of the factory town and of those enormous districts in every large city in which the children live who most need the protection of child labor legislation consists of people who have come together in response to the demands of modern industry and who are held together by the purely impersonal tie of working in one large factory, in which they not only do not know each other, but in which no one person nor even group of people, knows all of them. They are utterly without the natural and minute acquaintance and inter-family relationships which rural and village life affords, and are therefore much more dependent upon the social sympathy and power of effective association which is becoming its urban substitute. This substitute can be most easily experienced among groups of children.

Play is the great social stimulus, and it is the prime motive which unites children and draws them into comradeship. A true democratic relation and ease of acquaintance is found only among the children in a typical factory community because they readily overcome differences of language, tradition and religion, which form insuperable barriers to adults. "It is in play that nature reveals her anxious care to discover men to each other," and this happy and important task children unconsciously carry forward day by day with all the excitement and joy of co-ordinate activity. They accomplish that which their elders could not possibly do, and they render a most important service to the community. Social observers comment upon the influence of this group and gang spirit as it is carried over into politics, but no valuable observations have as yet been recorded of its relation to the present system of production, which is so pre-eminently one of large numbers of men working together for hours at a time, probably because the factory offers so little opportunity for its exercise compared to the operations of self-government even in its most unsatisfactory manifestations in a crowded city quarter.

It would bring a new power into modern industry if the factory could avail itself of that *esprit de corps*, that triumphant buoyancy which the child experiences when he feels his complete identification with a social group; that sense of security which comes upon him sitting in a theatre or "at a party" when he issues forth from himself and is lost in a fairyland which has been evoked not only by his own imagination, but by that of his companions as well. This power of association, of assimilation which children possess in such a high degree, is easily carried over into the affairs of youth if it but be given opportunity and freedom for action as it is in the college life of more favored young people. The *esprit de corps* of an athletic team, that astonishing force of co-operation, is, however, never consciously carried over into industry, and is persistently disregarded. It is indeed lost before it is discovered, if I may be permitted an Irish bull, in the case of children who are put to work before they have had time to develop the power beyond its most childish and haphazard manifestations.

Factory life depends upon groups of people working together, and yet it is content with the morphology of the group, as it were, paying no attention to its psychology to the interaction of its members. By regarding each producer as a solitary unit a tremendous power is totally unutilized, but in the case of children who are prematurely put to work under such conditions an unwarranted nervous strain is added as they make their effort to stand up to the individual duties of life while still in the stage of group and family dependence. We can all recall moments in our childhood when we were not allowed to go "out to play" with other children and were overcome with rage and helpless despair as we looked from the window at the playing group which we could not join. We can recall moments of even more bitter isolation when we were "with the others," but owing to some eccentricity of dress or some other stupid mistake of a controlling adult, we still felt quite outside of the group which we so fervently called our own. Some such remembrance may perhaps aid our imagination in behalf of the solitary child working in a crowded factory.

We naturally associate a factory with orderly productive action, but similarity of action without identical thought and co-operative intelligence is coercion and not order, and the present factory discipline needs to be redeemed as the old school discipline has been redeemed. In the latter the system of prizes and punishments has been given up not only because they were difficult to administer, but because they utterly failed to free the power of the child. "The fear of starvation," of which the old economists made so much, is, after all, but a poor incentive to work, and the appeal to cupidity by which a man is induced to "speed up" in all the various devices of piecework is very little better. The natural reaction against these in the determined efforts of workmen "to limit the output" has arraigned the entire system. It is the old revolt against incessant muscular labor divorced from any exercise of the instinct of workmanship and devoid of the creative touch of the artist.

Let us realize before it is too late that in this age of iron, of machine-tending, and of sub-divided labor, that we need, as never before, the untrammeled and inspired activity of youth. . . .

7

The Public School
and the Immigrant Child

Addams wrote frequently of the need to relate schools to other institutions — here she writes of their relationship to the immigrant family. Always concerned with the practical value of knowledge, she claims that schooling will be more meaningful to immigrant children if what they learn there enables them to help their parents to adapt to their new environment. Addams points out that efforts to facilitate the adjustment of adult immigrants will also help to preserve the family's capacity to fulfill its traditional socializing functions, which, in turn, will help to insure a smooth transition to adulthood for the young.

I am always diffident when I come before a professional body of teachers, realizing as I do that it is very easy for those of us who look on to bring indictments against results; and realizing also that one of the most difficult situations you have to meet is the care and instruction of the immigrant child, especially as he is found where I see him, in the midst of crowded city conditions.

And yet in spite of the fact that the public school is the great savior of the immigrant district, and the one agency which inducts the children into the changed conditions of American life, there is a certain indict-

SOURCE: National Education Association, *Journal of Proceedings and Addresses*, 1908, pp. 99–102.

ment which may justly be brought, in that the public school too often separates the child from his parents and widens that old gulf between fathers and sons which is never so cruel and so wide as it is between the immigrants who come to this country and their children who have gone to the public school and feel that they have there learned it all. The parents are thereafter subjected to certain judgment, the judgment of the young which is always harsh and in this instance founded upon the most superficial standard of Americanism. And yet there is a notion of culture which we would define as a knowledge of those things which have been long cherished by men, the things which men have loved because thru generations they have softened and interpreted life, and have endowed it with value and meaning. Could this standard have been given rather than the things which they see about them as the test of so-called success, then we might feel that the public school has given at least the beginnings of culture which the child ought to have. At present the Italian child goes back to its Italian home more or less disturbed and distracted by the contrast between the school and the home. If he throws off the control of the home because it does not represent the things which he has been taught to value he takes the first step toward the Juvenile Court and all the other operations of the law, because he has prematurely asserted himself long before he is ready to take care of his own affairs.

We find in the carefully prepared figures which Mr. Commons and other sociologists have published that while the number of arrests of immigrants is smaller than the arrests of native born Americans, the number

She's looking @ the systematic oppression w/ judicial system

of arrests among children of immigrants is twice as large as the number of arrests among the children of native born Americans. It would seem that in spite of the enormous advantages which the public school gives to these children it in some way loosens them from the authority and control of their parents, and tends to send them, without a sufficient rudder and power of self-direction, into the perilous business of living. Can we not say, perhaps, that the schools ought to do more to connect these children with the best things of the past, to make them realize something of the beauty and charm of the language, the history, and the traditions which their parents represent. It is easy to cut them loose from their parents, it requires cultivation to tie them up in sympathy and understanding. The ignorant teacher cuts them off because he himself cannot understand the situation, the cultivated teacher fastens them because his own mind is open to the charm and beauty of that old-country life. In short, it is the business of the school to give to each child the beginnings of a culture so wide and deep and universal that he can interpret his own parents and countrymen by a standard which is world-wide and not provincial.

The second indictment which may be brought is the failure to place the children into proper relation toward the industry which they will later enter. Miss Arnold has told us that children go into industry for a very short time. I believe that the figures of the United States census show the term to be something like six years for the women in industry as over against twenty-four years for men, in regard to continuity of service. Yet you cannot disregard the six years of the girls nor the twenty-four years of the boys, because they are the immediate occupation into which they enter after they leave the school — even the girls are bound to go thru that period — that is, the average immigrant girls are — before they enter the second serious business of life and maintain homes of their own. Therefore, if they enter industry unintelligently, without some notion of what it means, they find themselves totally unprepared for their first experience with American life, they are thrown out without the proper guide or clue which the public school might and ought to have given to them. Our industry has become so international, that it ought to be easy to use the materials it offers for immigrant children. The very processes and general principles which industry represents give a chance to prepare these immigrant children in a way which the most elaborated curriculum could not present. Ordinary material does not give the same international suggestion as industrial material does.

Third, I do not believe that the children who have been cut off from their own parents are going to be those who, when they become parents themselves, will know how to hold the family together and to connect it with the state. I should begin to teach the girls to be good mothers by teaching them to be good daughters. Take a girl whose mother has come from South Italy. The mother cannot adjust herself to the changed condition of housekeeping, does not know how to wash and bake here, and do the other things which she has always done well in Italy, because she has suddenly been transported from a village to a tenement house. If that girl studies these household conditions in relation to the past and to the present needs of the family, she is undertaking the very best possible preparation for her future obligations to a household of her own. And to my mind she can undertake it in no better way. Her own children are mythical and far away, but the little brothers and sisters pull upon her affections and her loyalty, and she longs to have their needs recognized in the school so that the school may give her some help. Her mother complains that the baby is sick in America because she cannot milk her own goat; she insists if she had her own goat's milk the baby would be quite well and flourishing, as the children were in Italy. If that girl can be taught that the milk makes the baby ill because it is not clean and be provided with a simple test that she may know when milk is clean, it may take her into the study not only of the milk within the four walls of the tenement house, but into the inspection of the milk of her district. The milk, however, remains good educational material, it makes even more concrete the connection which you would be glad to use between the household and the affairs of the American city. Let her not follow the mother's example of complaining about changed conditions; let her rather make the adjustment for her mother's entire household. We cannot tell what adjustments the girl herself will be called upon to make ten years from now; but we can give her the clue and the aptitude to adjust the family with which she is identified to the constantly changing conditions of city life. Many of us feel that, splendid as the public schools are in their relation to the immigrant child, they do not understand all of the difficulties which surround that child — all of the moral and emotional perplexities which constantly harass him. The children long that the school teacher should know something about the lives their parents lead and should be able to reprove the hooting children who make fun of the Italian mother because she wears a kerchief on her head, not only because they are rude but also because they are stupid. We send young people to Europe to see Italy, but we do not utilize Italy when it lies about the schoolhouse. If the body of teachers in our great cities could take hold of the immigrant colonies, could bring out of them their handicrafts and occupations, their traditions, their folk songs and folk lore, the beautiful stories which every immigrant colony is ready to tell and translate; could get the children to bring these things into school as the material from which culture is made and the material upon which culture is based, they would discover that by comparison that which they give them now is a poor meretricious and vulgar thing. Give these children a chance to utilize the historic and industrial material which they see about them and they will begin to have a sense of ease in America, a first consciousness of being at home. I believe if these people are welcomed upon the basis of the resources which they represent and the contributions which they bring, it may come to pass that these schools which deal with immigrants will find that they have a wealth of cultural and industrial material which will make the schools in other neighborhoods positively envious. A girl living in a tenement household, helping along this tremendous adjustment, healing over this great moral upheaval which the parents have suffered and which leaves them bleeding and sensitive — such a girl has a richer experience and a finer material than any girl from a more fortunate household can have at the present moment.

I wish I had the power to place before you what it

seems to me is the opportunity that the immigrant colonies present to the public school: the most endearing occupation of leading the little child, who will in turn lead his family, and bring them with him into the brotherhood for which they are longing. The immigrant child cannot make this demand upon the school because he does not know how to formulate it; it is for the teacher both to perceive it and to fulfil it.

8

The House of Dreams

This is an excerpt from The Spirit of Youth and the City Streets, *which Addams's nephew said was "of all her books the nearest to her heart" (Linn,* Jane Addams, *p. 178). It expresses her profound and sympathetic understanding of youthful idealism as well as her concern with the social, recreational, and even inspirational opportunities available to young men and women. Drama, music, and sport, she argues, have powerful, lasting effects on the behavior and development of young people. Just as the public has a responsibility for schooling, so too does it have a responsibility for the quality of the experiences young people find outside of school. If the impulses of the young are to be directed into healthful and socially useful activities, she suggests, public priorities must be developed to counter commercial priorities in entertainment. As is frequently the case, the specifics of Addams's argument may be dated—five-cent theaters having long since been displaced by television and other new media—and yet the essential question she poses—how shall we respond to the dreams of youth?—bears consideration still.*

To the preoccupied adult who is prone to use the city street as a mere passageway from one hurried duty to another, nothing is more touching than his encounter with a group of children and young people who are

SOURCE: *The Spirit of Youth and the City Streets* (New York: Macmillan, 1909), chap. 4. A slightly different version of this material that expands on Addams's view of the theater may be found in "The Reaction of Modern Life Upon Religious Education," *Religious Education* 4 (1909): 23–29.

emerging from a theater with the magic of the play still thick upon them. They look up and down the familiar street scarcely recognizing it and quite unable to determine the direction of home. From a tangle of "make believe" they gravely scrutinize the real world which they are so reluctant to reënter, reminding one of the absorbed gaze of a child who is groping his way back from fairy-land whither the story has completely transported him.

"Going to the show" for thousands of young people in every industrial city is the only possible road to the realms of mystery and romance; the theater is the only place where they can satisfy that craving for a conception of life higher than that which the actual world offers them. In a very real sense the drama and the drama alone performs for them the office of art as is clearly revealed in their blundering demand stated in many forms for "a play unlike life." The theater becomes to them a "veritable house of dreams" infinitely more real than the noisy streets and the crowded factories.

This first simple demand upon the theater for romance is closely allied to one more complex which might be described as a search for solace and distraction in those moments of first awakening from the glamour of a youth's interpretation of life to the sterner realities which are thrust upon his consciousness. These perceptions which inevitably "close around" and imprison the spirit of youth are perhaps never so grim as in the case of the wage-earning child. We can all recall our own moments of revolt against life's actualities, our reluctance to admit that all life was to be as unheroic and uneventful as that which we saw about us, it was too unbearable that "this was all there was" and we tried every possible avenue of escape. As we made an effort to believe, in spite of what we saw, that life was noble and harmonious, as we stubbornly clung to poesy in contradiction to the testimony of our senses, so we see thousands of young people thronging the theaters bent in their turn upon the same quest. The drama provides a transition between the romantic conceptions which they vainly struggle to keep intact and life's cruelties and trivialities which they refuse to admit. A child whose imagination has been cultivated is able to do this for himself through reading and reverie, but for the overworked city youth of meager education, perhaps nothing but the theater is able to perform this important office.

The theater also has a strange power to forecast life for the youth. Each boy comes from our ancestral past not "in entire forgetfulness," and quite as he unconsciously uses ancient war-cries in his street play, so he longs to reproduce and to see set before him the valors and vengeances of a society embodying a much more primitive state of morality than that in which he finds himself. . . . The elemental action which the stage presents, the old emotions of love and jealousy, of revenge and daring take the thoughts of the spectator back into deep and well worn channels in which his mind runs with a sense of rest afforded by nothing else. The cheap drama brings cause and effect, will power and action, once more into relation and gives a man the thrilling conviction that he may yet be master of his fate. The youth of course, quite unconscious of this psychology, views the deeds of the hero simply as a forecast of his own future and it is this fascinating view of his own career which draws the boy to "shows" of all sorts. They can scarcely be too improbable for him, portraying, as they do, his belief in his own prowess. A series of slides which has lately been very popular in the five-cent theaters of Chicago, portrayed five masked men breaking into a humble dwelling, killing the father of the family and carrying away the family treasure. The golden-haired son of the house, aged seven, vows eternal vengeance on the spot, and follows one villain after another to his doom. The execution of each is shown in lurid detail, and the last slide of the series depicts the hero, aged ten, kneeling upon his father's grave counting on the fingers of one hand the number of men that he has killed, and thanking God that he has been permitted to be an instrument of vengeance.

In another series of slides, a poor woman is wearily bending over some sewing, a baby is crying in the cradle, and two little boys of nine and ten are asking for food. In despair the mother sends them out into the street to beg, but instead they steal a revolver from a pawn shop and with it kill a Chinese laundryman, robbing him of $200. They rush home with the treasure which is found by the mother in the baby's cradle, whereupon she and her sons fall upon their knees and send up a prayer of thankfulness for this timely and heaven-sent assistance.

Is it not astounding that a city allows thousands of its youth to fill their impressionable minds with these absurdities which certainly will become the foundation for their working moral codes and the data from which they will judge the proprieties of life?

It is as if a child, starved at home, should be forced

to go out and search for food, selecting, quite naturally, not that which is nourishing but that which is exciting and appealing to his outward sense, often in his ignorance and foolishness blundering into substances which are filthy and poisonous.

Out of my twenty years' experience at Hull-House I can recall all sorts of pilferings, petty larcenies, and even burglaries, due to that never ceasing effort on the part of boys to procure theater tickets. I can also recall indirect efforts towards the same end which are most pitiful. I remember the remorse of a young girl of fifteen who was brought into the Juvenile Court after a night spent weeping in the cellar of her home because she had stolen a mass of artificial flowers with which to trim a hat. She stated that she had taken the flowers because she was afraid of losing the attention of a young man whom she had heard say that "a girl has to be dressy if she expects to be seen." This young man was the only one who had ever taken her to the theater and if he failed her, she was sure that she would never go out again, and she sobbed out incoherently that she "couldn't live at all without it." Apparently the blankness and grayness of life itself had been broken for her only by the portrayal of a different world.

One boy whom I had known from babyhood began to take money from his mother from the time he was seven years old, and after he was ten she regularly gave him money for the play Saturday evening. However, the Saturday performance, "starting him off like," he always went twice again on Sunday, procuring the money in all sorts of illicit ways. Practically all of his earnings after he was fourteen were spent in this way to satisfy the insatiable desire to know of the great

adventures of the wide world which the more fortunate
boy takes out in reading Homer and Stevenson.

In talking with his mother, I was reminded of my
experience one Sunday afternoon in Russia when the
employees of a large factory were seated in an open-air
theater, watching with breathless interest the presentation of folk stories. I was told that troupes of actors
went from one manufacturing establishment to another presenting the simple elements of history and
literature to the illiterate employees. This tendency to
slake the thirst for adventure by viewing the drama
is, of course, but a blind and primitive effort in the
direction of culture, for "he who makes himself its
vessel and bearer thereby acquires a freedom from the
blindness and soul poverty of daily existence."

It is partly in response to this need that more sophis-
ticated young people often go to the theater, hoping
to find a clue to life's perplexities. Many times the
bewildered hero reminds one of Emerson's description
of Margaret Fuller, "I don't know where I am going,
follow me"; nevertheless, the stage is dealing with the
moral themes in which the public is most interested.

And while many young people go to the theater if
only to see represented, and to hear discussed, the
themes which seem to them so tragically important,
there is no doubt that what they hear there, flimsy and
poor as it often is, easily becomes their actual moral
guide. In moments of moral crisis they turn to the sayings of the hero who found himself in a similar plight.
The sayings may not be profound, but at least they
are applicable to conduct. In the last few years scores
of plays have been put upon the stage whose titles
might be easily translated into proper headings for
sociological lectures or sermons, without including the

plays of Ibsen, Shaw and Hauptmann, which deal so directly with moral issues that the moralists themselves wince under their teachings and declare them brutal. But it is this very brutality which the over-refined and complicated city dwellers often crave. Moral teaching has become so intricate, creeds so metaphysical, that in a state of absolute reaction they demand definite instruction for daily living. Their whole-hearted acceptance of the teaching corroborates the statement recently made by an English playwright that "The theater is literally making the minds of our urban populations today. It is a huge factory of sentiment, of character, of points of honor, of conceptions of conduct, of everything that finally determines the destiny of a nation. The theater is not only a place of amusement, it is a place of culture, a place where people learn how to think, act, and feel." Seldom, however, do we associate the theater with our plans for civic righteousness, although it has become so important a factor in city life.

One Sunday evening last winter an investigation was made of four hundred and sixty six theaters in the city of Chicago, and it was discovered that in the majority of them the leading theme was revenge; the lover following his rival; the outraged husband seeking his wife's paramour; or the wiping out by death of a blot on a hitherto unstained honor. It was estimated that one sixth of the entire population of the city had attended the theaters on that day. At that same moment the churches throughout the city were preaching the gospel of good will. Is not this a striking commentary upon the contradictory influences to which the city youth is constantly subjected?

This discrepancy between the church and the stage

is at times apparently recognized by the five-cent theater itself, and a blundering attempt is made to suffuse the songs and moving pictures with piety. Nothing could more absurdly demonstrate this attempt than a song, illustrated by pictures, describing the adventures of a young man who follows a pretty girl through street after street in the hope of "snatching a kiss from her ruby lips." The young man is overjoyed when a sudden wind storm drives the girl to shelter under an archway, and he is about to succeed in his attempt when the good Lord, "ever watchful over innocence," makes the same wind "blow a cloud of dust into the eyes of the rubberneck," and "his foul purpose is foiled." This attempt at piety is also shown in a series of films depicting Bible stories and the Passion Play at Oberammergau, forecasting the time when the moving film will be viewed as a mere mechanical device for the use of the church, the school and the library, as well as for the theater.

At present, however, most improbable tales hold the attention of the youth of the city night after night, and feed his starved imagination as nothing else succeeds in doing. In addition to these fascinations, the five-cent theater is also fast becoming the general social center and club house in many crowded neighborhoods. It is easy of access from the street, the entire family of parents and children can attend for a comparatively small sum of money, and the performance lasts for at least an hour; and, in some of the humbler theaters, the spectators are not disturbed for a second hour.

The room which contains the mimic stage is small and cozy, and less formal than the regular theater, and there is much more gossip and social life as if the foyer and pit were mingled. The very darkness of the room, necessary for an exhibition of the films, is an added attraction to many young people, for whom the space is filled with the glamour of love making.

Hundreds of young people attend these five-cent theaters every evening in the week, including Sunday, and what is seen and heard there becomes the sole topic of conversation, forming the ground pattern of their social life. That mutual understanding which in another social circle is provided by books, travel and all the arts, is here compressed into the topics suggested by the play.

The young people attend the five-cent theaters in groups, with something of the "gang" instinct, boasting of the films and stunts in "our theater." They find a certain advantage in attending one theater regularly, for the *habitués* are often invited to come upon the stage on "amateur nights," which occur at least once a week in all the theaters. This is, of course, a most exciting experience. If the "stunt" does not meet with the approval of the audience, the performer is greeted with jeers and a long hook pulls him off the stage; if, on the other hand, he succeeds in pleasing the audience, he may be paid for his performance and later register with a booking agency, the address of which is supplied by the obliging manager, and thus he fancies that a lucrative and exciting career is opening before him. Almost every night at six o'clock a long line of children may be seen waiting at the entrance of these booking agencies, of which there are fifteen that are well known in Chicago.

Thus, the only art which is constantly placed before

the eyes of "the temperamental youth" is a debased
form of dramatic art, and a vulgar type of music, for
the success of a song in these theaters depends not so
much upon its musical rendition as upon the vulgarity
of its appeal. In a song which held the stage of a cheap
theater in Chicago for weeks, the young singer was
helped out by a bit of mirror from which she threw
a flash of light into the faces of successive boys whom
she selected from the audience as she sang the refrain,
"You are my Affinity." Many popular songs relate the
vulgar experiences of a city man wandering from an
amusement park to bathing beach in search of flirta-
tions. It may be that these "stunts" and recitals of city
adventure contain the nucleus of coming poesy and
romance, as the songs and recitals of the early min-
strels sprang directly from the life of the people, but
all the more does the effort need help and direction,
both in the development of its technique and the material of its themes.

The few attempts which have been made in this
direction are astonishingly rewarding to those who
regard the power of self-expression as one of the most
precious boons of education. The Children's Theater
in New York is the most successful example, but every
settlement in which dramatics have been systematically
fostered can also testify to a surprisingly quick response
to this form of art on the part of young people. The
Hull-House Theater is constantly besieged by children
clamoring to "take part" in the plays of Schiller, Shakespeare, and Molière, although they know it means
weeks of rehearsal and the complete memorizing of
"stiff" lines. The audiences sit enthralled by the final
rendition and other children whose tastes have sup-

posedly been debased by constant vaudeville, are pa-
thetically eager to come again and again. Even when
still more is required from the young actors, research
into the special historic period, copying costumes from
old plates, hours of labor that the "th" may be restored
to its proper place in English speech, their enthusiasm
is unquenched. But quite aside from its educational
possibilities one never ceases to marvel at the power
of even a mimic stage to afford to the young a magic
space in which life may be lived in efflorescence, where
manners may be courtly and elaborate without exciting ridicule, where the sequence of events is impressive
and comprehensible. Order and beauty of life is what
the adolescent youth craves above all else as the younger child indefatigably demands his story. "Is this where
the most beautiful princess in the world lives?" asks
a little girl peering into the door of the Hull-House
Theater, or "Does Alice in Wonderland always stay
here?" It is much easier for her to put her feelings into
words than it is for the youth who has enchantingly
rendered the gentle poetry of Ben Jonson's "Sad
Shepherd," or for him who has walked the boards as
Southey's Wat Tyler. His association, however, is
quite as clinging and magical as is the child's although
he can only say, "Gee, I wish I could always feel the
way I did that night. Something would be doing then."
Nothing of the artist's pleasure, nor of the revelation
of that larger world which surrounds and completes
our own, is lost to him because a careful technique has
been exacted, — on the contrary this has only dignified
and enhanced it. It would also be easy to illustrate
youth's eagerness for artistic expression from the recitals given by the pupils of the New York Music

School Settlement, or by those of the Hull-House Music School. These attempts also combine social life with the training of the artistic sense and in this approximate the fascinations of the five-cent theater.

This spring a group of young girls accustomed to the life of a five-cent theater, reluctantly refused an invitation to go to the country for a day's outing because the return on a late train would compel them to miss one evening's performance. They found it impossible to tear themselves away not only from the excitements of the theater itself but from the gaiety of the crowd of young men and girls invariably gathered outside discussing the sensational posters.

A steady English shopkeeper lately complained that unless he provided his four daughters with the money for the five-cent theaters every evening they would steal it from his till, and he feared that they might be driven to procure it in even more illicit ways. Because his entire family life had been thus disrupted he gloomily asserted that "this cheap show had ruined his 'ome and was the curse of America." This father was able to formulate the anxiety of many immigrant parents who are absolutely bewildered by the keen absorption of their children in the cheap theater. This anxiety is not, indeed, without foundation. An eminent alienist of Chicago states that he has had a number of patients among neurotic children whose emotional natures have been so over-wrought by the crude appeal to which they had been so constantly subjected in the theaters, that they have become victims of hallucination and mental disorder. The statement of this physician may be the first note of alarm which will awaken the city to its duty in regard to the theater, so that it shall at least be made safe and sane for the city child whose senses are already so abnormally developed.

This testimony of a physician that the conditions are actually pathological, may at last induce us to bestir ourselves in regard to procuring a more wholesome form of public recreation. Many efforts in social amelioration have been undertaken only after such exposures; in the meantime, while the occasional child is driven distraught, a hundred children permanently injure their eyes watching the moving films, and hundreds more seriously model their conduct upon the standards set before them on this mimic stage.

Three boys, aged nine, eleven and thirteen years, who had recently seen depicted the adventures of frontier life including the holding up of a stage coach and the lassoing of the driver, spent weeks planning to lasso, murder, and rob a neighborhood milkman, who started on his route at four o'clock in the morning. They made their headquarters in a barn and saved enough money to buy a revolver, adopting as their watchword the phrase "Dead Men Tell no Tales." One spring morning the conspirators, with their faces covered with black cloth, lay "in ambush" for the milkman. Fortunately for him, as the lariat was thrown the horse shied, and, although the shot was appropriately fired, the milkman's life was saved. Such a direct influence of the theater is by no means rare, even among older boys. Thirteen young lads were brought into the Municipal Court in Chicago during the first week that "Raffles, the Amateur Cracksman" was upon the stage, each one with an outfit of burglar's tools in his possession, and each one shamefacedly admitting that the gentlemanly burglar in the play had suggested to him a career of similar adventure.

In so far as the illusions of the theater succeed in giving youth the rest and recreation which comes from following a more primitive code of morality, it has a close relation to the function performed by public games. It is, of course, less valuable because the sense of participation is largely confined to the emotions and the imagination, and does not involve the entire nature.

We might illustrate by the "Wild West Show" in which the onlooking boy imagines himself an active participant. The scouts, the Indians, the bucking ponies, are his real intimate companions and occupy his entire mind. In contrast with this we have the omnipresent game of tag which is, doubtless, also founded upon the chase. It gives the boy exercise and momentary echoes of the old excitement, but it is barren of suggestion and quickly degenerates into horse-play.

Well considered public games easily carried out in a park or athletic field, might both fill the mind with the imaginative material constantly supplied by the theater, and also afford the activity which the cramped muscles of the town dweller so sorely need. Even the unquestioned ability which the theater possesses to bring men together into a common mood and to afford them a mutual topic of conversation, is better accomplished with the one national game which we already possess, and might be infinitely extended through the organization of other public games.

The theater even now by no means competes with the baseball league games which are attended by thousands of men and boys who, during the entire summer, discuss the respective standing of each nine and the relative merits of every player. During the noon hour all the employees of a city factory gather in the nearest vacant lot to cheer their own home team in its practice for the next game with the nine of a neighboring manufacturing establishment and on a Saturday afternoon the entire male population of the city betakes itself to the baseball field; the ordinary means of transportation are supplemented by gay stage-coaches and huge automobiles, noisy with blowing horns and decked with gay pennants. The enormous crowd of cheering men and boys are talkative, good-natured, full of the holiday spirit, and absolutely released from the grind of life. They are lifted out of their individual affairs and so fused together that a man cannot tell whether it is his own shout or another's that fills his ears; whether it is his own coat or another's that he is wildly waving to celebrate a victory. He does not call the stranger who sits next to him his "brother" but he unconsciously embraces him in an overwhelming outburst of kindly feeling when the favorite player makes a home run. Does not this contain a suggestion of the undoubted power of public recreation to bring together all classes of a community in the modern city unhappily so full of devices for keeping men apart?

Already some American cities are making a beginning toward more adequate public recreation. Boston has its municipal gymnasiums, cricket fields, and golf grounds. Chicago has seventeen parks with playing fields, gymnasiums and baths, which at present enroll thousands of young people. These same parks are provided with beautiful halls which are used for many purposes, rent free, and are given over to any group

of young people who wish to conduct dancing parties
subject to city supervision and chaperonage. Many
social clubs have deserted neighboring saloon halls for
these municipal drawing rooms beautifully decorated
with growing plants supplied by the park greenhouses,
and flooded with electric lights supplied by the park
power house. In the saloon halls the young people were
obliged to "pass money freely over the bar," and in
order to make the most of the occasion they usually
stayed until morning. At such times the economic
necessity itself would override the counsels of the more
temperate, and the thrifty door keeper would not insist
upon invitations but would take in any one who had
the "price of a ticket." The free rent in the park hall,
the good food in the park restaurant, supplied at cost,
have made three parties closing at eleven o'clock no
more expensive than one party breaking up at day-
light, too often in disorder.

Is not this an argument that the drinking, the late
hours, the lack of decorum, are directly traceable to
the commercial enterprise which ministers to pleasure
in order to drag it into excess because excess is more
profitable? To thus commercialize pleasure is as mon-
strous as it is to commercialize art. It is intolerable that
the city does not take over this function of making provision for pleasure, as wise communities in Sweden
and South Carolina have taken the sale of alcohol out
of the hands of enterprising publicans.

We are only beginning to understand what might
be done through the festival, the street procession, the
band of marching musicians, orchestral music in
public squares or parks, with the magic power they
all possess to formulate the sense of companionship

and solidarity. The experiments which are being made in public schools to celebrate the national holidays, the changing seasons, the birthdays of heroes, the planting of trees, are slowly developing little ceremonials which may in time work out into pageants of genuine beauty and significance. No other nation has so unparalleled an opportunity to do this through its schools as we have, for no other nation has so widespreading a school system, while the enthusiasm of children and their natural ability to express their emotions through symbols, gives the securest possible foundation to this growing effort.

The city schools of New York have effected the organization of high school girls into groups for folk dancing. These old forms of dancing which have been worked out in many lands and through long experiences, safeguard unwary and dangerous expression and yet afford a vehicle through which the gaiety of youth may flow. Their forms are indeed those which lie at the basis of all good breeding, forms which at once express and restrain, urge forward and set limits.

One may also see another center of growth for public recreation and the beginning of a pageantry for the people in the many small parks and athletic fields which almost every American city is hastening to provide for its young. These small parks have innumerable athletic teams, each with its distinctive uniform, with track meets and match games arranged with the teams from other parks and from the public schools; choruses of trade unionists or of patriotic societies fill the park halls with eager listeners. Labor Day processions are yearly becoming more carefully planned and more picturesque in character, as the desire to make

an overwhelming impression with mere size gives way
to a growing ambition to set forth the significance of
the craft and the skill of the workman. At moments
they almost rival the dignified showing of the processions of the German Turn Vereins which are also often
seen in our city streets.

The many foreign colonies which are found in all
American cities afford an enormous reserve of material
for public recreation and street festival. They not only
celebrate the feasts and holidays of the fatherland, but
have each their own public expression for their mutual
benefit societies and for the observance of American
anniversaries. From the gay celebration of the Scandi-
navians when war was averted and two neighboring
nations were united, to the equally gay celebration of
the centenary of Garibaldi's birth; from the Chinese
dragon cleverly trailing its way through the streets, to
the Greek banners flung out in honor of immortal
heroes, there is an infinite variety of suggestions and
possibilities for public recreation and for the corporate
expression of stirring emotions. After all, what is the
function of art but to preserve in permanent and beautiful form those emotions and solaces which cheer life
and make it kindlier, more heroic and easier to com-
prehend; which lift the mind of the worker from the
harshness and loneliness of his task, and, by connect-
ing him with what has gone before, free him from a
sense of isolation and hardship?

Were American cities really eager for municipal art,
they would cherish as genuine beginnings the tarantella
danced so interminably at Italian weddings; the primitive Greek pipe played throughout the long summer
nights; the Bohemian theaters crowded with eager

Slavophiles; the Hungarian musicians strolling from street to street; the fervid oratory of the young Russian preaching social righteousness in the open square.

Many Chicago citizens who attended the first annual meeting of the National Playground Association of America, will never forget the long summer day in the large playing field filled during the morning with hundreds of little children romping through the kindergarten games, in the afternoon with the young men and girls contending in athletic sports; and the evening light made gay by the bright colored garments of Italians, Lithuanians, Norwegians, and a dozen other nationalities, reproducing their old dances and festivals for the pleasure of the more stolid Americans. Was this a forecast of what we may yet see accomplished through a dozen agencies promoting public recreation which are springing up in every city of America, as they already are found in the large towns of Scotland and England?

Let us cherish these experiments as the most precious beginnings of an attempt to supply the recreational needs of our industrial cities. To fail to provide for the recreation of youth, is not only to deprive all of them of their natural form of expression, but is certain to subject some of them to the overwhelming temptation of illicit and soul-destroying pleasures. To insist that young people shall forecast their rose-colored future only in a house of dreams, is to deprive the real world of that warmth and reassurance which it so sorely needs and to which it is justly entitled; furthermore, we are left outside with a sense of dreariness, in company with that shadow which already lurks only around the corner for most of us — a skepticism of life's value.

9

Immigrants
and Their Children

Addams's concern about intergenerational conflict in immigrant families, combined with the value she saw in cultural continuity as a source for social progress, led to one of the settlement's most innovative educational experiments, the Hull House Labor Museum. As this description of the museum indicates, it provided a means for preserving traditional craft skills, the hope being to enable immigrant parents to display and transmit to their children the dignity they had once derived from their work.

An overmastering desire to reveal the humbler immigrant parents to their own children lay at the base of what has come to be called the Hull-House Labor Museum. This was first suggested to my mind one early spring day when I saw an old Italian woman, her distaff against her homesick face, patiently spinning a thread by the simple stick spindle so reminiscent of all southern Europe. I was walking down Polk Street, perturbed in spirit, because it seemed so difficult to come into genuine relations with the Italian women and because they themselves so often lost their hold upon their Americanized children. It seemed to me that Hull-House ought to be able to devise some educational enterprise, which should build a bridge between European and American experiences in such

SOURCE: *Twenty Years at Hull-House* (New York: Macmillan, 1910), chap. 11.

wise as to give them both more meaning and a sense of relation. I meditated that perhaps the power to see life as a whole, is more needed in the immigrant quarter of a large city than anywhere else, and that the lack of this power is the most fruitful source of misunderstanding between European immigrants and their children, as it is between them and their American neighbors; and why should that chasm between fathers and sons, yawning at the feet of each generation, be made so unnecessarily cruel and impassable to these bewildered immigrants? Suddenly I looked up and saw the old woman with her distaff, sitting in the sun on the steps of a tenement house. She might have served as a model for one of Michael Angelo's Fates, but her face brightened as I passed and, holding up her spindle for me to see, she called out that when she had spun a little more yarn, she would knit a pair of stockings for her goddaughter. The occupation of the old woman gave me the clew that was needed. Could we not interest the young people working in the neighboring factories, in these older forms of industry, so that, through their own parents and grandparents, they would find a dramatic representation of the inherited resources of their daily occupation. If these young people could actually see that the complicated machinery of the factory had been evolved from simple tools, they might at least make a beginning towards that education which Dr. Dewey defines as "a continuing reconstruction of experience." They might also lay a foundation for reverence of the past which Goethe declares to be the basis of all sound progress.

My exciting walk on Polk Street was followed by many talks with Dr. Dewey and with one of the teachers in his school who was a resident at Hull-House. Within a month a room was fitted up to which we might invite those of our neighbors who were possessed of old crafts and who were eager to use them.

We found in the immediate neighborhood, at least four varieties of these most primitive methods of spinning and three distinct variations of the same spindle in connection with wheels. It was possible to put these seven into historic sequence and order and to connect the whole with the present method of factory spinning. The same thing was done for weaving, and on every Saturday evening a little exhibit was made of these various forms of labor in the textile industry. Within one room a Syrian woman, a Greek, an Italian, a Russian, and an Irishwoman enabled even the most casual observer to see that there is no break in orderly evolution if we look at history from the industrial standpoint; that industry develops similarly and peacefully year by year among the workers of each nation, heedless of differences in language, religion, and political experiences.

And then we grew ambitious and arranged lectures upon industrial history. I remember that after an interesting lecture upon the industrial revolution in England and a portrayal of the appalling conditions throughout the weaving districts of the north, which resulted from the hasty gathering of the weavers into the new towns, a Russian tailor in the audience was moved to make a speech. He suggested that whereas time had done much to alleviate the first difficulties in the transition of weaving from hand work to steam power, that in the application of steam to sewing we are still in the first stages, illustrated by the isolated woman who tries to support herself by hand needlework at home until driven out by starvation, as many of the hand weavers had been.

The historical analogy seemed to bring a certain comfort to the tailor as did a chart upon the wall, showing the infinitesimal amount of time that steam had been applied to manufacturing processes compared to the centuries of hand labor. Human progress is slow and perhaps never more cruel than in the advance of industry, but is not the worker comforted by knowing that other historical periods have existed similar to the one in which he finds himself, and that the readjustment may be shortened and alleviated by judicious action; and is he not entitled to the solace which an artistic portrayal of the situation might give him? I remember the evening of the tailor's speech that I felt reproached because no poet or artist has endeared the sweaters' victim to us as George Eliot has made us love the belated weaver, Silas Marner. The textile museum is connected directly with the basket weaving, sewing, millinery, embroidery, and dressmaking constantly being taught at Hull-House, and so far as possible with the other educational departments; we have also been able to make a collection of products, of early implements, and of photographs which are full of suggestion. Yet far beyond its direct educational value, we prize it because it so often puts the immigrants into the position of teachers, and we imagine that it affords them a pleasant change from the tutelage in which all Americans, including their own children, are so apt to hold them. I recall a number of Russian women working in a sewing-room near Hull-House, who heard one Christmas week that the House was going to give a party to which they might come. They arrived one afternoon when, unfortunately, there was no party on hand and, although the residents did their best to entertain them with impromptu music and refreshments, it was quite evident that they were greatly disappointed. Finally it was suggested that they be shown the Labor Museum — where gradually the thirty sodden, tired women were transformed. They knew how to use the spindles and were delighted to find the Russian spinning frame. Many of them had never seen the spinning wheel, which has not penetrated to certain parts of Russia, and they regarded it as a new and wonderful invention. They turned up their dresses to show their homespun petticoats; they tried the looms; they explained the difficulty of the old patterns; in short, from having been stupidly entertained, they themselves did the entertaining. Because of a direct appeal to former experiences, the immigrant visitors were able for the moment to instruct their American hostesses in an old and honored craft, as was indeed becoming to their age and experience.

Russian
women seeing
a spinning wheel

In some such ways as these have the Labor Museum and the shops pointed out the possibilities which Hull-House has scarcely begun to develop, of demonstrating that culture is an understanding of the long-established occupations and thoughts of men, of the arts with which they have solaced their toil. A yearning to recover for the household arts something of their early sanctity and meaning, arose strongly within me one evening when I was attending a Passover Feast to which I had been invited by a Jewish family in the neighborhood, where the traditional and religious significance of woman's daily activity was still retained.

immigrants
educated
americans
on their
culture

The kosher food the Jewish mother spread before her family had been prepared according to traditional knowledge and with constant care in the use of utensils; upon her had fallen the responsibility to make all ready according to Mosaic instructions that the great crisis in a religious history might be fittingly set forth by her husband and son. Aside from the grave religious significance in the ceremony, my mind was filled with shifting pictures of woman's labor with which travel makes one familiar; the Indian women grinding grain outside of their huts as they sing praises to the sun and rain; a file of white-clad Moorish women whom I had once seen waiting their turn at a well in Tangiers; south Italian women kneeling in a row along the stream and beating their wet clothes against the smooth white stones; the milking, the gardening, the marketing in thousands of hamlets, which are such direct expressions of the solicitude and affection at the basis of all family life.

There has been some testimony that the Labor Museum has revealed the charm of woman's primitive activities. I recall a certain Italian girl who came every Saturday evening to a cooking class in the same building in which her mother spun in the Labor Museum exhibit; and yet Angelina always left her mother at the front door while she herself went around to a side door because she did not wish to be too closely identified in the eyes of the rest of the cooking class with an Italian woman who wore a kerchief over her head, uncouth boots, and short petticoats. One evening, however, Angelina saw her mother surrounded by a group of visitors from the School of Education, who much admired the spinning, and she concluded from their conversation that her mother was "the best stick-spin-dler spinner in America." When she inquired from me as to the truth of this deduction, I took occasion to describe the Italian village in which her mother had lived, something of her free life, and how, because of the opportunity she and the other women of the village had to drop their spindles over the edge of a precipice, they had developed a skill in spinning beyond that of the neighboring towns. I dilated somewhat on the free-dom and beauty of that life — how hard it must be to exchange it all for a two-room tenement, and to give up a beautiful homespun kerchief for an ugly depart-ment store hat. I intimated it was most unfair to judge her by these things alone, and that while she must de-pend on her daughter to learn the new ways, she also had a right to expect her daughter to know something of the old ways.

That which I could not convey to the child but upon which my own mind persistently dwelt, was that her mother's whole life had been spent in a secluded spot under the rule of traditional and narrowly localized observances, until her very religion clung to local sanc-tities, — to the shrine before which she had always prayed, to the pavement and walls of the low vaulted church, — and then suddenly she was torn from it all and literally put out to sea, straight away from the solid habits of her religious and domestic life, and she now walked timidly but with poignant sensibility upon a new and strange shore.

It was easy to see that the thought of her mother with any other background than that of the tenement was new to Angelina and at least two things resulted; she allowed her mother to pull out of the big box under the bed the beautiful homespun garments which had been previously hidden away as uncouth; and she openly came into the Labor Museum by the same door as did her mother, proud at least of the mastery of the craft which had been so much admired.

A club of necktie workers formerly meeting at Hull-House, persistently resented any attempt on the part of their director to improve their minds. The president once said that she "wouldn't be caught dead at a lecture," that she came to the club "to get some fun out of it," and indeed it was most natural that she should crave recreation after a hard day's work. One evening I saw the entire club listening to quite a stiff lecture in the Labor Museum and to my rather wicked remark to the president that I was surprised to see her enjoying a lecture, she replied, that she did not call this a lecture, she called this "getting next to the stuff you work with all the time." It was perhaps the sincerest tribute we have ever received as to the success of the undertaking.

The Labor Museum continually demanded more space as it was enriched by a fine textile exhibit lent by the Field Museum, and later by carefully selected specimens of basketry from the Philippines. The shops have finally included a group of three or four women, Irish, Italian, Danish, who have become a permanent working force in the textile department which has developed into a self-supporting industry through the sale of its homespun products.

These women and a few men, who come to the museum to utilize their European skill in pottery, metal, and wood, demonstrate that immigrant colonies might yield to our American life something very valuable, if their resources were intelligently studied and developed. I recall an Italian, who had decorated the doorposts of his tenement with a beautiful pattern he had previously used in carving the reredos of a Neapolitan church, who was "fired" by his landlord on the ground of destroying property. His feelings were hurt, not so much that he had been put out of his house, as that his work had been so disregarded; and he said that when people traveled in Italy they liked to look at wood carvings but that in America "they only made money out of you." *exhorting*

Sometimes the suppression of the instinct of workmanship is followed by more disastrous results. A Bohemian whose little girl attended classes at Hull-House, in one of his periodic drunken spells had literally almost choked her to death, and later had committed suicide when in delirium tremens. His poor wife, who stayed a week at Hull-House after the disaster until a new tenement could be arranged for her, one day showed me a gold ring which her husband had made for their betrothal. It exhibited the most exquisite workmanship, and she said that although in the old country he had been a goldsmith, in America he had for twenty years shoveled coal in a furnace room of a large manufacturing plant; that whenever she saw one of his "restless fits," which preceded his drunken periods, "coming on," if she could provide him with a bit of metal and persuade him to stay at home and work at it, he was all right and the time passed without disaster, but that "nothing else would do it." This story threw a flood of light upon the dead man's struggle and on the stupid maladjustment which had broken him down. Why had we never been told? Why had our interest in the remarkable musical ability of his child, blinded us to the hidden artistic ability of the father? We had forgotten that a long-established occupation may form the very foundations of the moral life, that the art with which a man has solaced his toil may be the salvation of his uncertain temperament.

10

Socialized Education

Here Addams describes some of the more formal educational activities at Hull House. She also restates her belief that education can be both practical and enlivening and that it must be available to people of all social classes.

. . . Hull-House in the very beginning opened what we called College Extension Classes with a faculty finally numbering thirty-five college men and women, many of whom held their pupils for consecutive years. As these classes antedated in Chicago the University Extension and Normal Extension classes and supplied a demand for stimulating instruction, the attendance strained to their utmost capacity the spacious rooms in the old house. The relation of students and faculty to each other and to the residents was that of guest and hostess and at the close of each term the residents gave a reception to students and faculty which was one of the chief social events of the season. Upon this comfortable social basis some very good work was done.

In connection with these classes a Hull-House summer school was instituted at Rockford College, which was most generously placed at our disposal by the trustees. For ten years one hundred women gathered there for six weeks, in addition there were always men on the faculty, and a small group of young men among

SOURCE: *Twenty Years at Hull-House* (New York: Macmillan, 1910), chap. 18.

172

the students who were lodged in the gymnasium building. The outdoor classes in bird study and botany, the serious reading of literary masterpieces, the boat excursions on the Rock River, the coöperative spirit of doing the housework together, the satirical commencements in parti-colored caps and gowns, lent themselves toward a reproduction of the comradeship which college life fosters.

As each member of the faculty, as well as the students, paid three dollars a week, and as we had little outlay beyond the actual cost of food, we easily defrayed our expenses. The undertaking was so simple and gratifying in results that it might well be reproduced in many college buildings which are set in the midst of beautiful surroundings, unused during the two months of the year, when hundreds of people, able to pay only a moderate price for lodgings in the country, can find nothing comfortable and no mental food more satisfying than piazza gossip.

Every Thursday evening during the first years, a public lecture came to be an expected event in the neighborhood, and Hull-House became one of the early University Extension centers, first in connection with an independent society and later with the University of Chicago. One of the Hull-House trustees was so impressed with the value of this orderly and continuous presentation of economic subjects that he endowed three courses in a downtown center, in which the lectures were free to any one who chose to come. He was much pleased that these lectures were largely attended by workingmen who ordinarily prefer that an economic subject shall be presented by a partisan, and who are supremely indifferent to examinations and credits. They also dislike the balancing of pro and con which scholarly instruction implies, and prefer to be "inebriated on raw truth" rather than to sip a carefully prepared draught of knowledge.

Nevertheless Bowen Hall, which seats seven hundred and fifty people, is often none too large to hold the audiences of men who come to Hull-House every Sunday evening during the winter to attend the illustrated lectures provided by the faculty of the University of Chicago, and others who kindly give their services. These courses differ enormously in their popularity: one on European capitals and their social significance was followed with the most vivid attention and sense of participation indicated by groans and hisses when the audience was reminded of an unforgettable feud between Austria and her Slavic subjects, or when they wildly applauded a Polish hero endeared through his tragic failure.

In spite of the success of these Sunday evening courses, it has never been an easy undertaking to find acceptable lecturers. A course of lectures on astronomy illustrated by stereopticon slides will attract a large audience the first week, who hope to hear of the wonders of the heavens and the relation of our earth thereto, but instead are treated to spectrum analyses of star dust, or the latest theory concerning the milky way. The habit of research and the desire to say the latest word upon any subject often overcomes the sympathetic understanding of his audience which the lecturer might otherwise develop, and he insensibly drops into the dull terminology of the classroom. There are, of course, notable exceptions; we had twelve gloriously popular talks on organic evolution, but the lecturer was not yet a professor — merely a university instructor — and his mind was still eager over the marvel of it all. Fortunately there are an increasing number of lecturers whose matter is so real, so definite and so valuable, that in an attempt to give it an exact equivalence in words, they utilize the most direct forms of expression.

It sometimes seems as if the men of substantial scholarship were content to leave to the charlatan the teaching of those things which deeply concern the welfare of mankind, and that the mass of men get their intellectual food from the outcasts of scholarship, who provide millions of books, pictures, and shows, not to instruct and guide, but for the sake of their own financial profit. A Settlement soon discovers that simple people are interested in large and vital subjects and the Hull-House residents themselves at one time, with only partial success, undertook to give a series of lectures on the history of the world, beginning with the nebular hypothesis and reaching Chicago itself in the twenty-fifth lecture! Absurd as the hasty review appears, there is no doubt that the beginner in knowledge is always eager for the general statement, as those wise old teachers of the people well knew, when they put the history of creation on the stage and the monks themselves became the actors.

. . . The residents of Hull-House place increasing emphasis upon the great inspirations and solaces of literature and are unwilling that it should ever languish as a subject for class instruction or for reading parties. The Shakespeare club has lived a continuous existence at Hull-House for sixteen years during which time its members have heard the leading interpreters of Shake-

speare, both among scholars and players. I recall that
one of its earliest members said that her mind was
peopled with Shakespeare characters during her long
hours of sewing in a shop, that she couldn't remember
what she thought about before she joined the club, and
concluded that she hadn't thought about anything at
all. To feed the mind of the worker, to lift it above the
monotony of his task, and to connect it with the larger
world, outside of his immediate surroundings, has
always been the object of art, perhaps never more
nobly fulfilled than by the great English bard. Miss
Starr has held classes in Dante and Browning for many
years and the great lines are conned with never failing
enthusiasm. I recall Miss Lathrop's Plato club and an
audience who listened to a series of lectures by Dr.
John Dewey on "Social Psychology," as genuine intellectual groups consisting largely of people from the
immediate neighborhood, who were willing to make
"that effort from which we all shrink, the effort of
thought." But while we prize these classes as we do the
help we are able to give to the exceptional young man
or woman who reaches the college and university and
leaves the neighborhood of his childhood behind him,
the residents of Hull-House feel increasingly that the
educational efforts of a Settlement should not be directed primarily to reproduce the college type of culture, but to work out a method and an ideal adapted
to the immediate situation. They feel that they should
promote a culture which will not set its possessor aside
in a class with others like himself, but which will, on
the contrary, connect him with all sorts of people by
his ability to understand them as well as by his power
to supplement their present surroundings with the

historic background. Among the hundreds of immigrants who have for years attended classes at Hull-House designed primarily to teach the English language, dozens of them have struggled to express in the newly acquired tongue some of those hopes and longings which had so much to do with their emigration.

A series of plays was thus written by a young Bohemian; essays by a Russian youth, outpouring sorrows rivaling Werther himself and yet containing the precious stuff of youth's perennial revolt against accepted wrong; stories of Russian oppression and petty injustices throughout which the desire for free America became a crystallized hope; an attempt to portray the Jewish day of Atonement, in such wise that even individualistic Americans may catch a glimpse of that deeper national life which has survived all transplanting and expresses itself in forms so ancient that they appear grotesque to the ignorant spectator. I remember a pathetic effort on the part of a young Russian Jewess to describe the vivid inner life of an old Talmud scholar, probably her uncle or father, as of one persistently occupied with the grave and important things of the spirit, although when brought into sharp contact with busy and overworked people, he inevitably appeared self-absorbed and slothful. Certainly no one who had read her paper could again see such an old man in his praying shawl bent over his crabbed book, without a sense of understanding.

On the other hand, one of the most pitiful periods in the drama of the much-praised young American who attempts to rise in life, is the time when his educational requirements seem to have locked him up and made him rigid. He fancies himself shut off from his uneducated family and misunderstood by his friends. He is bowed down by his mental accumulations and often gets no farther than to carry them through life as a great burden, and not once does he obtain a glimpse of the delights of knowledge.

The teacher in a Settlement is constantly put upon his mettle to discover methods of instruction which shall make knowledge quickly available to his pupils .... Even a meager knowledge of English may mean an opportunity to work in a factory *versus* nonemployment, or it may mean a question of life or death when a sharp command must be understood in order to avoid the danger of a descending crane.

In response to a demand for an education which should be immediately available, classes have been established and grown apace in cooking, dressmaking, and millinery. A girl who attends them will often say that she "expects to marry a workingman next spring," and because she has worked in a factory so long she knows "little about a house." Sometimes classes are composed of young matrons of like factory experiences. I recall one of them whose husband had become so desperate after two years of her unskilled cooking that he had threatened to desert her and go where he could get "decent food," as she confided to me in a tearful interview, when she followed my advice to take the Hull-House courses in cooking, and at the end of six months reported a united and happy home.

Two distinct trends are found in response to these classes; the first is for domestic training, and the other is for trade teaching which shall enable the poor little milliner and dressmaker apprentices to shorten the two years of errand running which is supposed to teach them their trade.

The beginning of trade instruction has been already evolved in connection with the Hull-House Boys' club. The ample Boys' club building presented to Hull-House three years ago by one of our trustees has afforded well-equipped shops for work in wood, iron, and brass; for smithing in copper and tin; for commercial photography, for printing, for telegraphy, and electrical construction. These shops have been filled with boys who are eager for that which seems to give them a clew to the industrial life all about them. These classes meet twice a week and are taught by intelligent workingmen who apparently give the boys what they want better than do the strictly professional teachers. While these classes in no sense provide a trade training, they often enable a boy to discover his aptitude and help him in the selection of what he "wants to be" by reducing the trades to embryonic forms. The factories are so complicated that the boy brought in contact with them, unless he has some preliminary preparation, is apt to become confused. In pedagogical terms, he loses his "power of orderly reaction" and is often so discouraged or so overstimulated in his very first years of factory life that his future usefulness is seriously impaired.

One of Chicago's most significant experiments in the direction of correlating the schools with actual industry was for several years carried on in a public school building situated near Hull-House, in which the bricklayers' apprentices were taught eight hours a day in special classes during the non-bricklaying season. This early public school venture anticipated the very successful arrangement later carried on in Cincinnati, in Pittsburg, and in Chicago itself, whereby a group of boys at work in a factory alternate month by month with another group who are in school and are thus intelligently conducted into the complicated processes of modern industry. But for a certain type of boy who has been demoralized by the constant change and excitement of street life, even these apprenticeship classes are too strenuous, and he has to be lured into the path of knowledge by all sorts of appeals.

It sometimes happens that boys are held in the Hull-House classes for weeks by their desire for the excitement of placing burglar alarms under the door mats. But to enable the possessor of even a little knowledge to thus play with it, is to decoy his feet at least through the first steps of the long, hard road of learning, although even in this, the teacher must proceed warily. A typical street boy who was utterly absorbed in a wood-carving class, abruptly left never to return when he was told to use some simple calculations in the laying out of the points. He evidently scented the approach of his old enemy, arithmetic, and fled the field. On the other hand, we have come across many cases in which boys have vainly tried to secure such opportunities for themselves. During the trial of a boy of ten recently arrested for truancy, it developed that he had spent many hours watching the electrical construction in a downtown building, and many others in the public library "reading about electricity." Another boy who was taken from school early, when his father lost both of his legs in a factory accident, tried in vain to find a place for himself "with machinery." He was declared too small for any such position, and for four years worked as an errand boy, during which time he steadily turned in his unopened pay envelope for the use of the household. At the end of the fourth year the boy disappeared, to the great distress of his invalid father and his poor mother whose day washings became the sole support of the family. He had beaten his way to Kansas City, hoping "they wouldn't be so particular there about a fellow's size." He came back at the end of six weeks because he felt sorry for his mother who, aroused at last to a realization of his unbending purpose, applied for help to the Juvenile Protective Association. They found a position for the boy in a machine shop and an opportunity for evening classes.

Out of the fifteen hundred members of the Hull-House Boys' club, hundreds seem to respond only to the opportunities for recreation, and many of the older ones apparently care only for the bowling and the billiards. And yet tournaments and match games under supervision and regulated hours are a great advance over the sensual and exhausting pleasures to be found so easily outside the club. These organized sports readily connect themselves with the Hull-House gymnasium and with all those enthusiasms which are so mysteriously aroused by athletics.

Our gymnasium has been filled with large and enthusiastic classes for eighteen years in spite of the popularity of dancing and other possible substitutes, while the Saturday evening athletic contests have become a feature of the neighborhood. The Settlement strives for that type of gymnastics which is at least partly a matter of character, for that training which presupposes abstinence and the curbing of impulse, as well as for those athletic contests in which the mind of the contestant must be vigilant to keep the body closely to the rules of the game. As one sees in rhythmic motion the slim bodies of a class of lads, "that scru-

pulous and uncontaminate purity of form which rec-
ommended itself even to the Greeks as befitting messengers from the gods, if such messengers should come,"
one offers up in awkward prosaic form the very essence
of that old prayer, "Grant them with feet so light to
pass through life." But while the glory stored up for
Olympian winners was at most a handful of parsley,
an ode, fame for family and city, on the other hand,
when the men and boys from the Hull-House gymnasium bring back their cups and medals, one's mind
is filled with something like foreboding in the reflec-
tion that too much success may lead the winners into
that professionalism which is so associated with bet-
ting and so close to pugilism. Candor, however, com-
pels me to state that a long acquaintance with the
acrobatic folk who have to do with the circus, a large
number of whom practice in our gymnasium every
winter, has raised our estimate of that profession.

Young people who work long hours at sedentary occupations, factories and offices, need perhaps more
than anything else the freedom and ease to be acquired
from a symmetrical muscular development and are
quick to respond to that fellowship which athletics apparently afford more easily than anything else. The
Greek immigrants form large classes and are eager to
reproduce the remnants of old methods of wrestling,
and other bits of classic lore which they still possess,
and when one of the Greeks won a medal in a wrestling
match which represented the championship of the entire city, it was quite impossible that he should present it to the Hull-House trophy chest without a classic
phrase which he recited most gravely and charming-
ly. . . .

Before closing this chapter on Socialized Education, it is only fair to speak of the education accruing to the Hull-House residents themselves during their years of living in what at least purports to be a center for social and educational activity.

While a certain number of the residents are primarily interested in charitable administration and the amelioration which can be suggested only by those who know actual conditions, there are other residents identified with the House from its earlier years to whom the groups of immigrants make the historic appeal, and who use, not only their linguistic ability, but all the resource they can command of travel and reading to qualify themselves for intelligent living in the immigrant quarter of the city. I remember one resident lately returned from a visit in Sicily, who was able to interpret to a bewildered judge the ancient privilege of a jilted lover to scratch the cheek of his faithless sweetheart with the edge of a coin. Although the custom in America had degenerated into a knife slashing after the manner of foreign customs here, and although the Sicilian deserved punishment, the incident was yet lifted out of the slough of mere brutal assault, and the interpretation won the gratitude of many Sicilians.

There is no doubt that residents in a Settlement too often move towards their ends "with hurried and ignoble gait," putting forth thorns in their eagerness to bear grapes. It is always easy for those in pursuit of ends which they consider of overwhelming importance to become themselves thin and impoverished in spirit and temper, to gradually develop a dark mistaken eagerness alternating with fatigue, which supersedes "the great and gracious ways" so much more congruous with worthy aims.

Partly because of this universal tendency, partly because a Settlement shares the perplexities of its times and is never too dogmatic concerning the final truth, the residents would be glad to make the daily life at the Settlement "conform to every shape and mode of excellence."

It may not be true

> "That the good are always the merry
> Save by an evil chance,"

but a Settlement would make clear that one need not be heartless and flippant in order to be merry, nor solemn in order to be wise. Therefore quite as Hull-House tries to redeem billiard tables from the association of gambling, and dancing from the temptations of the public dance halls, so it would associate with a life of upright purpose those more engaging qualities which in the experience of the neighborhood are too often connected with dubious aims. . . .

The Settlement casts aside none of those things which cultivated men have come to consider reasonable and goodly, but it insists that those belong as well to that great body of people who, because of toilsome and underpaid labor, are unable to procure them for themselves. Added to this is a profound conviction that the common stock of intellectual enjoyment should not be difficult of access because of the economic position of him who would approach it, that those "best results of civilization" upon which depend the finer and freer aspects of living must be incorporated into our common life and have free mobility through all elements of society if we would have our democracy endure.

The educational activities of a Settlement, as well as its philanthropic, civic, and social undertakings, are but differing manifestations of the attempt to socialize democracy, as is the very existence of the Settlement itself.

11

Recreation as a Public Function in Urban Communities

In this article Addams links her earlier arguments concerning public responsibility for recreation (see selection 8, "The House of Dreams") to two of her central political concerns: respect for ethnic and national diversity as a basis for "Americanism" and "good government."

If the city would preserve for its inhabitants the greatest gift in its possession — that which alone justifies the existence of the city — the opportunity for varied and humanizing social relationships, it must undertake more fully than it has yet done to provide centers in which social life may be organized and carried on steadily and normally. A fair argument may be made for the contention that this provision is a public function. It may even be charged that it is a solemn obligation of the modern heterodox city.

In the old city-states, such as Athens or Florence, local emotion could be depended upon to hold the citizens in a common bond. Each man could imagine that all his fellow-citizens were like himself and could draw from a fund of similar experiences. The area of government corresponded to the area of acquaintance, or at least to that of memory and filial piety. Such a basis of patriotism held as late as the time of Bismarck,

SOURCE: American Sociological Society, *Proceedings* 6 (1911): 35–39. Reprinted in *American Journal of Sociology* 17 (1912): 615–619.

for instance, who when he founded his great German Empire was eager to obtain Saxony and Hanover because he thought they could be easily assimilated to the Prussian type, while he was doubtful of Bavaria because he considered it too Austrian. Mazzini, in spite of his great humanitarianism, also believed that the New Italy must be held together by the similarity of the various states to a special national type. But in the modern city, and especially the cities in America, solidarity cannot depend upon any of these sanctions, for the state is composed of people brought together from all the nations of the earth. The patriotism of the modern state must be based not upon a consciousness of homogeneity but upon a respect for variation, not upon inherited memory but upon trained imagination.

The scientists tell us that the imaginative powers, the sense that life possesses variety and color, are realized most easily in moments of pleasure and recreation. Social intercourse must be depended upon that men may be brought together through comradeship into a mood which discovers and respects this quality of human difference and variation. As immigrants to America work together in factories, every effort is made that they should conform to a common standard; as they walk upon the street they make painful exertion to approach a prevailing mode in dress; only on the playground or in the recreation center do they find that variety is prized, that distinctive folklore and national customs as well as individual initiative are at a premium. They meet together and enjoy each other's national dances and games, and as the sense of comradeship and pleasure grows, they are able to express, as nowhere else, that sense of being unlike one's fellows which is at the basis of all progress. They meet in the kingdom of the mind — in the empire of imagination — as they discover that folk customs are similar in all nations. In the play festivals of Chicago sustained in the various small parks, the Italians, Poles, Lithuanians, and Norwegians meet each other with a dignity and freedom, with a sense of comradeship, which they are unable to command at any other time.

There is no doubt that the future patriotism of America must depend not so much upon conformity as upon respect for variety, and nowhere can this be inculcated as it can in the public recreation centers.

There are yet other arguments for recreation as a public function: I have lived for many years in Chicago in a ward which has been represented in the Common Council by an alderman who is considered notoriously corrupt. I have always been interested in his methods of procedure, and I was much startled some years ago, when Hull House was conducting a campaign against him, to be told by a wise man in the locality that such an alderman could never be defeated save by a candidate who had grown up in the ward and had a long experience in a gang. I have since learned to understand what he meant. The leader of a gang of boys gains his prestige largely through his power of obtaining favors for his followers. He discovers the alley in which they may play a game of craps undisturbed because the policeman is willing to pretend not to see them; he later finds the poolrooms in which minors may congregate undisturbed in defiance of the law, the saloons which easily and readily sell liquor to minors, or the gambling places which are protected by obscure yet powerful influences. It is but a step farther when he and his followers are voters, and he is running for office, to extend the same kind of protection to all of the men who are "faithful." They will have special privileges of all sorts given through his bounty, and he will be able to protect them from the operations of any law which may prove to be inconvenient to them. He merely continues on a larger scale the excellent training he had in the gang, and continues to utilize those old human motives — personal affection, desire for favors, fear of ridicule, and loyalty to comrades.

While the power of a politician of this type is being rapidly abridged by the establishment of civil service in cities as well as by the operations of the various efficiency bureaus, to my mind it is being broken into more rapidly from the other end, as it were, by the gradual abolition of this particular type of gang training through the establishment of public recreation centers. A group of boys will not continue to stand upon the street corners and to seek illicit pleasures in alleys and poolrooms when all the fascinating apparatus of a recreation field is at their disposal. When such a gang enters the recreation field, the leader finds that this special power of manipulation which he has developed is of no use there. The business of the superintendent of the recreation center is to see that each gang of boys is fairly treated, that the "liberty of each is limited by the like liberty of all" — to use an old Spencerian phrase. The boy who is admired is not he who can secure secret favors, but the one who can best meet those standards which boys maintain of running, climbing, turning, etc. They may seem like absurd standards to the adult, but they are at least universal standards, with the competition open to all and dependent upon personal prowess. The leader of the gang may or may not shine on the athletic field, and the boys who are there learn to resist exploitation; they come to despise and to bring opprobrium to bear upon any comrade who wishes to receive special favors either for himself or his fellows. A rude sort of justice prevails — very important, because boys who have no opportunity to put in practice such notions of justice as they have when they are boys, it is safe to predict, will not resent social injustice when they grow to be men. The opportunity which the athletic field provides for discussion of actual events and for comradeship founded upon the establishment of just relationships is the basis for a new citizenship and in the end will overthrow the corrupt politician. In fact, I see no other way of overthrowing him in a crowded city quarter where people's prejudices are easily played upon, except this open-air, widespread opportunity for social intercourse when the boys are still young and full of initiative and enthusiasm. If girls were voting, I would of course say the same thing for them.

After all, a city is made up of an infinitely varying multitude, working their way, through much pain and confusion, toward juster human relations, which are indeed the ideal political relations. These must be expressed first in social intercourse, and discussed with freedom and energy, if progress is to be made. The very size of the city sometimes intensifies this intercourse into a pathological condition, but nevertheless it is all the more necessary to put it under the direction of skilled instructors and to provide places where it may be carried on normally.

The fifteen Small Parks of Chicago, equipped with

clubrooms, poolrooms, drawing-rooms, refectories, reading-rooms, gymnasiums, swimming-pools, and much other social paraphernalia, are, we believe, centers in which a higher type of citizenship is being nursed. Certainly the number of arrests among juvenile delinquents falls off surprisingly in a neighborhood where such a park has been established — a negative measure, possibly, but one which cannot be disregarded. As the temple of the Greeks inspired the youth's patriotism, and as the city walls conserved but at the same time limited his imagination, so, we hope, these centers of public recreation, simply because they stand for high comradeship and intercourse, will inspire American youth to a sense of political obligation, while at the same time they teach him that the kingdom of the mind is without boundary and that he may find patriotic relationship with the youth of all nations.

12

Moral Education
and Legal Protection
for Children

Prostitution troubled many reformers in the early twentieth century, Addams among them. Here she writes of the circumstances that lead young people into "commercialized vice" and calls for a variety of corrective measures, including sex education in the public schools and legislative action to protect juvenile rights. Urging more extensive child-labor regulation and full state support of "mothers' pensions," which would allow working women to remain at home to supervise their children, Addams argues that city children will only receive the protection they need and deserve when the state concerns itself with all "educational forces."

No great wrong has ever arisen more clearly to the social consciousness of a generation than has that of commercialized vice in the consciousness of ours, and that we are slow to act is simply another evidence that human nature has a curious power of callous indifference towards evils which have been so entrenched that they seem part of that which has always been. Educators of course share this attitude; at moments they seem to intensify it, although at last an educational movement in the direction of sex hygiene is beginning

SOURCE: *A New Conscience and an Ancient Evil* (New York: Macmillan, 1912), chap. 4. Reprinted in *McClure's Magazine* 38 (1912): 338–344.

in the schools and colleges. Primary schools strive to satisfy the child's first questionings regarding the beginnings of human life and approach the subject through simple biological instruction which at least places this knowledge on a par with other natural facts. Such teaching is an enormous advance for the children whose curiosity would otherwise have been satisfied from poisonous sources and who would have learned of simple physiological matters from such secret undercurrents of corrupt knowledge as to have forever perverted their minds. Yet this first direct step towards an adequate educational approach to this subject has been surprisingly difficult owing to the self-consciousness of grown-up people; for while the children receive the teaching quite simply, their parents often take alarm. . . .

. . . All the great religions of the world have recognized youth's need of spiritual help during the trying years of adolescence. The ceremonies of the earliest religions deal with this instinct almost to the exclusion of others, and all later religions attempt to provide the youth with shadowy weapons for the struggle which lies ahead of him, for the wise men in every age have known that only the power of the spirit can overcome the lusts of the flesh. In spite of this educational advance, courses of study in many public and private schools are still prepared exactly as if educators had never known that at fifteen or sixteen years of age, the will power being still weak, the bodily desires are keen and insistent. The head master of Eton, Mr. Lyttleton, who has given much thought to this gap in the education of youth says, "The certain result of leaving an enormous majority of boys unguided and uninstructed

in a matter where their strongest passions are concerned, is that they grow up to judge of all questions
connected with it, from a purely selfish point of view."
He contends that this selfishness is due to the fact that
any single suggestion or hint which boys receive on
the subject comes from other boys or young men who
are under the same potent influences of ignorance,
curiosity and the claims of self. No wholesome coun-
ter-balance of knowledge is given, no attempt is made
to invest the subject with dignity or to place it in relation to the welfare of others and to universal law. Mr.
Lyttleton contends that this alone can explain the
peculiarly brutal attitude towards "outcast" women
which is a sustained cruelty to be discerned in no other
relation of English life. To quote him again: "But when
the victims of man's cruelty are not birds or beasts but
our own countrywomen, doomed by the hundred thousand to a life of unutterable shame and hopeless misery,
then and then only the general average tone of young
men becomes hard and brutally callous or frivolous
with a kind of coarse frivolity not exhibited in relation
to any other form of human suffering." At the present
moment thousands of young people in our great cities
possess no other knowledge of this grave social evil
which may at any moment become a dangerous personal menace, save what is imparted to them in this
brutal flippant spirit. It has been said that the child
growing up in the midst of civilization receives from
its parents and teachers something of the accumulated
experience of the world on all other subjects save upon
that of sex. On this one subject alone each generation
learns little from its predecessors.

An educator has lately pointed out that it is an old

lure of vice to pretend that it alone deals with manliness and reality, and he complains that it is always difficult to convince youth that the higher planes of life contain anything but chilly sentiments. He contends that young people are therefore prone to receive moralizing and admonitions with polite attention, but when it comes to action, they carefully observe the life about them in order to conduct themselves in such wise as to be part of the really desirable world inhabited by men of affairs. Owing to this attitude, many young people living in our cities at the present moment have failed to apprehend the admonitions of religion and have never responded to its inner control. It is as if the impact of the world had stunned their spiritual natures, and as if this had occurred at the very time that a most dangerous experiment is being tried. The public gaieties formerly allowed in Catholic countries where young people were restrained by the confessional, are now permitted in cities where this restraint is altogether unknown to thousands of young people, and only faintly and traditionally operative upon thousands of others. The puritanical history of American cities assumes that these gaieties are forbidden, and that the streets are sober and decorous for conscientious young men and women who need no external protection. This ungrounded assumption, united to the fact that no adult has the confidence of these young people, who are constantly subjected to a multitude of imaginative impressions, is almost certain to result disastrously.

The social relationships in a modern city are so hastily made and often so superficial, that the old human restraints of public opinion, long sustained in smaller communities, have also broken down. Thousands of young men and women in every great city have received none of the lessons in self-control which even savage tribes imparted to their children when they taught them to master their appetites as well as their emotions. These young people are perhaps further from all community restraint and genuine social control than the youth of the community have ever been in the long history of civilization. Certainly only the modern city has offered at one and the same time every possible stimulation for the lower nature and every opportunity for secret vice. Educators apparently forget that this unrestrained stimulation of young people, so characteristic of our cities, although developing very rapidly, is of recent origin, and that we have not yet seen the outcome. The present education of the average young man has given him only the most unreal protection against the temptations of the city. Schoolboys are subjected to many lures from without just at the moment when they are filled with an inner tumult which utterly bewilders them and concerning which no one has instructed them save in terms of empty precept and unintelligible warning.

We are authoritatively told that the physical difficulties are enormously increased by uncontrolled or perverted imaginations, and all sound advice to young men in regard to this subject emphasizes a clean mind, exhorts an imagination kept free from sensuality and insists upon days filled with wholesome athletic interests. We allow this régime to be exactly reversed for thousands of young people living in the most crowded and most unwholesome parts of the city. Not only does the stage in its advertisements exhibit all the allurements of sex to such an extent that a play without a "love interest" is considered foredoomed to failure, but the novels which form the sole reading of thousands of young men and girls deal only with the course of true or simulated love, resulting in a rose-colored marriage, or in variegated misfortunes.

Often the only recreation possible for young men and young women together is dancing, in which it is always easy to transgress the proprieties. In many public dance halls, however, improprieties are deliberately fostered. The waltzes and two-steps are purposely slow, the couples leaning heavily on each other barely move across the floor, all the jollity and bracing exercise of the peasant dance is eliminated, as is all the careful decorum of the formal dance. The efforts to obtain pleasure or to feed the imagination are thus converged upon the senses which it is already difficult for young people to understand and to control. It is therefore not remarkable that in certain parts of the city groups of idle young men are found whose evil imaginations have actually inhibited their power for normal living. On the streets or in the poolrooms where they congregate their conversation, their tales of adventure, their remarks upon women who pass by, all reveal that they have been caught in the toils of an instinct so powerful and primal that when left without direction it can easily overwhelm its possessor and swamp his faculties. These young men, who do no regular work, who expect to be supported by their mothers and sisters and to get money for the shows and theatres by any sort of disreputable undertaking, are in excellent training for the life of the procurer, and it is from such groups that they are recruited. . . .

Could the imaginations of these young men have been controlled and cultivated, could the desire for adventure have been directed into wholesome channels, could these idle boys have been taught that, so far from being manly they were losing all virility, could higher interests have been aroused and standards given them in relation to this one aspect of life, the entire situation of commercialized vice would be a different thing.

The girls with a desire for adventure seem confined to this one dubious outlet even more than the boys, although there are only one-eighth as many delinquent girls as boys brought into the juvenile court in Chicago, the charge against the girls in almost every instance involves a loss of chastity. One of them who was vainly endeavoring to formulate the causes of her downfall, concentrated them all in the single statement that she wanted the other girls to know that she too was a "good Indian." Such a girl, while she is not an actual member of a gang of boys, is often attached to one by so many loyalties and friendships that she will seldom testify against a member, even when she has been injured by him. She also depends upon the gang when she requires bail in the police court or the protection that comes from political influence, and she is often very proud of her quasi-membership. The little girls brought into the juvenile court are usually daughters of those poorest immigrant families living in the worst type of city tenements, who are frequently forced to take boarders in order to pay the rent. A surprising number of little girls have first become involved in wrongdoing through the men of their own households. A recent inquiry among 130 girls living in a sordid red light district disclosed the fact that a majority of them had thus been victimized and the wrong had come to them so early that they had been despoiled at an average age of eight years. . . .

. . . Many mothers, hard pressed by poverty, are obliged to rent houses next to vicious neighborhoods and their children very early become familiar with all the outer aspects of vice. Among them are the children of widows who make friends with their dubious neighbors during the long days while their mothers are at work. . . .

. . . The recent Illinois law, providing that the children of widows may be supported by public funds paid to the mother upon order of the juvenile court, will eventually restore a mother's care to these poor children; but in the meantime, even the poor mother who is receiving such aid, in her forced search for cheap rent may be continually led nearer to the notoriously evil districts. . . .

. . . The children of the poorest colored families . . . are often forced to live in disreputable neighborhoods because they literally cannot rent houses anywhere else. Both because rents are always high for colored people and because the colored mothers are obliged to support their children, seven times as many of them, in proportion to their entire number, as of the white mothers, the actual number of colored children neglected in the midst of temptation is abnormally large. So closely is child life founded upon the imitation of what it sees that the child who knows all evil is almost sure in the end to share it. Colored children seldom roam far from their own neighborhoods: in the public playgrounds, which are theoretically open to them, they are made so uncomfortable by the slights

of other children that they learn to stay away, and,
shut out from legitimate recreation, are all the more
tempted by the careless, luxurious life of a vicious
neighborhood. In addition to the colored girls who
have thus from childhood grown familiar with the
outer aspects of vice, are others who are sent into the
district in the capacity of domestic servants by unscru-
pulous employment agencies who would not venture
to thus treat a white girl. The community forces the
very people who have confessedly the shortest history
of social restraint, into a dangerous proximity with the
vice districts of the city. This results, as might easily
be predicted, in a very large number of colored girls
entering a disreputable life. The negroes themselves
believe that the basic cause for the high percentage of
colored prostitutes is the recent enslavement of their
race with its attendant unstable marriage and parental
status, and point to thousands of slave sales that but
two generations ago disrupted the negroes' attempts
at family life. Knowing this as we do, it seems all the
more unjustifiable that the nation which is responsible
for the broken foundations of this family life should
carelessly permit the negroes, making their first struggle towards a higher standard of domesticity, to be
subjected to the most flagrant temptations which our
civilization tolerates. . . .

Even children who live in respectable neighborhoods
and are guarded by careful parents so that their imaginations are not perverted, but only starved, constantly conduct a search for the magical and impossible
which leads them into moral dangers. An astonishing
number of them consult palmists, soothsayers, and for-
tune tellers. These dealers in futurity, who sell only

love and riches, the latter often dependent upon the first, are sometimes in collusion with disreputable houses, and at the best make the path of normal living more difficult for their eager young patrons. There is something very pathetic in the sheepish, yet radiant, faces of the boy and girl, often together, who come out on the street from a dingy doorway which bears the palmist's sign of the spread-out hand. This remnant of primitive magic is all they can find with which to feed their eager imaginations, although the city offers libraries and galleries, crowned with man's later imaginative achievements. One hard-working girl of my acquaintance, told by a palmist that "diamonds were coming to her soon," afterwards accepted without a moment's hesitation a so-called diamond ring from a man whose improper attentions she had hitherto withstood.

In addition to these heedless young people, pulled into a sordid and vicious life through their very search for romance, are many little children ensnared by means of the most innocent playthings and pleasures of childhood. Perhaps one of the saddest aspects of the social evil as it exists to-day in the modern city, is the procuring of little girls who are too young to have received adequate instruction of any sort and whose natural safeguard of modesty and reserve has been broken down by the overcrowding of a tenement house life. Any educator who has made a careful study of the children from the crowded districts is impressed with the numbers of them whose moral natures are apparently unawakened. While there are comparatively few of these non-moral children in any one neighborhood, in the entire city their number is far from

negligible. Such children are used by disreputable people to invite their more normal playmates to house parties, which they attend again and again, lured by candy
and fruit, until they gradually learn to trust the vicious
hostess. . . . Such children, when brought to the psy-
chopathic clinic attached to the Chicago juvenile court,
are sometimes found to have incipient epilepsy or
other physical disabilities from which their conduct
may be at least partially accounted for. Sometimes
they come from respectable families, but more often
from families where they have been mistreated and
where dissolute parents have given them neither affection nor protection. Many of these children whose
relatives have obviously contributed to their delinquency are helped by the enforcement of the adult delinquency law.

One looks upon these hardened little people with
a sense of apology that educational forces have not
been able to break into their first ignorance of life
before it becomes toughened into insensibility, and one
knows that, whatever may be done for them later, because of this early neglect, they will probably always
remain impervious to the gentler aspects of life, as if
vice seared their tender minds with red-hot irons. Our
public-school education is so nearly universal, that if
the entire body of the teachers seriously undertook to
instruct all American youth in regard to this most important aspect of life, why should they not in time train
their pupils to continence and self-direction, as they
already discipline their minds with knowledge in regard to many other matters? Certainly the extreme
youth of the victims of the white slave traffic, both boys

and girls, places a great responsibility upon the educational forces of the community. . . .

Unquestionably the average American child has received a more expensive education than has yet been accorded to the child of any other nation. The girls working in department stores have been in the public schools on an average of eight years, while even the factory girls, who so often leave school from the lower grades, have yet averaged six and two-tenths years of education at the public expense, before they enter industrial life. Certainly the community that has accomplished so much could afford them help and oversight for six and a half years longer, which is the average length of time that a working girl is employed. The state might well undertake this, if only to secure its former investment and to save that investment from utter loss.

Our generation, said to have developed a new enthusiasm for the possibilities of child life, and to have put fresh meaning into the phrase "children's rights," may at last have the courage to insist upon a child's right to be well born and to start in life with its tiny body free from disease. . . .

. . . A sense of justice outraged by the wanton destruction of new-born children, may in time unite with that ardent tide of rising enthusiasm for the nurture of the young, until the old barriers of silence and inaction, behind which the social evil has so long intrenched itself, shall at last give way. . . .

13

Widening the Circle
of Enlightenment:
Hull House and Adult Education

*In this article Addams again writes about the functions of a
settlement, focusing particularly on some of the pedagogical
techniques developed at Hull House. Many of these represent
an extension of Deweyan concepts into the field of adult education, and all embody Addams's belief in the importance of
reciprocity as a basis for education and other forms of social
exchange.*

I remember in the early days of settlements — my mind
seems to be going back to early days a good deal — we
used to say that the settlement had a distinct place in
the educational field. We were bold enough to com-
pare ourselves with universities and colleges.

It was the business of the universities, we said, to
carry on research, to nibble away at the things we did
not know. They were to reduce the black region of ignorance by bringing to light pieces of information that
increased the sum total of human knowledge.

It was the business of the colleges, broadly speaking,
to hand down the knowledge that had thus been accumulated. Each succeeding generation would add to
the accumulation and help to build up our social traditions and our civilization.

SOURCE: *Journal of Adult Education* 2 (1930): 276–279.

It was the business of the settlements to do something unlike either of these things. It was the function of the settlements to bring into the circle of knowledge and fuller life, men and women who might otherwise be left outside.

Some of these men and women were outside simply because of their ignorance, some of them because they led lives of hard work that narrowed their interests, and others because they were unaware of the possibilities of life and needed a friendly hand to awaken them. The colleges and universities had made a little inner circle of illuminated space beyond which there stretched a region of darkness, and it was the duty of the settlements to draw some of those who were in the outer darkness into the light. It seemed to us that our mission was just as important as those of either the universities or the colleges.

It is easy for young settlements, as it is for all youth, to be boastful. It is easy to say what you are going to do before you have had a chance to try. But I still think that there was something fine in that youthful ideal, though often enough in the early days — and later — we have wondered whether we were accomplishing it.

II

In the beginning at Hull House we were surrounded by a great many Italians. Those were the days when unified Italy was still comparatively new and many of the Italians in our neighborhood had taken part in the great movement for unification. In our first Hull House reading club of foreign-born students we tried to read in English Mazzini's *On The Duties of Man*. It was very good reading but not always easy reading. Yet never in all my teaching have I had a more interesting class than that class of Italians. When we had finished reading *On The Duties of Man*, the class gave Hull House a bust of Mazzini — perhaps in gratitude that the course was over! At least I am quite sure that that was one of the motives for the gift.

I think that that experience gave us the clue to the proper method for teaching the foreign born. The thing to do is to discuss their own problems with them. In order to do this the teachers must themselves acquire an understanding of those problems. It is useless to pretend an interest that is not real, for the pretense is always found out, but a shared interest that is genuine is the best possible thing to use as the basis for discussions in a study class.

Hull House was started in April, 1889. Three years later a great massacre occurred at Kirschnereff, Russia. A large number of Russians of Jewish origin came to this country, and hundreds and hundreds of them settled in the neighborhood of our House. Partly because of our personal contacts with some of the Russians and partly because of our knowledge of the fineness of these people who had been persecuted and driven away from their own country, we felt an enormous interest in the whole Russian situation. We were also concerned with the effect upon our national existence of the sudden impulsion of a large number of persons who might easily be filled with hatred and a spirit of revenge. It was most important that we should help them to make a fresh start.

I read with a group of those Russians a book by

Tolstoi, in which he works out cogently his theory of nonresistance. When I think of that group I have an impression of something very vivid. They had an intense desire to master the English language because they had something very vital to say, and could not say it unless they could find the English words with which to express their meaning. It is surprising what a stimulus such a situation provides!

I remember once in our old social science club, before the theory of evolution became as generally accepted as it was later, a man stood up and said that he did not understand this theory of evolution, and another man who did not understand it any too well, I am afraid, told him what it was.

"You see, a lot of fish are swimming in a stream, and the stream overflows and they get stranded on the bank. Some of the fish lie down and die, just as easy as that, but some of them struggle to get back and they dig their fins into the sand and they fill their mouths with air, and they do everything they can to get back into the water. After a time, their fins turn into legs and their lungs get used to air and, lo and behold, they are frogs!"

I think something like that does happen in a measure when you are studying a language, not for the sake of studying it, but because you want to say something that you feel must be said, and must be said here and now.

A great many Greeks came to our ward at one time in the early nineties and we tried very hard to give them the beginnings of English. The Greeks as a rule are not illiterate. They have had compulsory education in Greece for a great number of years. Our Greeks

almost all read their own language and they were very
eager to learn to read and write English. It was impossible to seat them around tables in informal groups,
so we used to fill our theater with them and teach from
stereopticon views. As they looked at the pictures they
would shout out explanations of them in English: "This
man is buying a railroad ticket" — "This man is asking
for work" and so forth and so on. It was a very superficial kind of teaching but it broke through the ice, and
our students were less afraid to try their English with
large numbers of people than they would have been
in a small group, just as some of us like best to sing
in a large chorus.

The teaching of languages, especially in settlements,
ought to be kept socialized. Learning a foreign language is often a very dreary process. At Hull House
we made a practice for a great many years of having
parties several times during the winter; to which the
members of our classes were invited, and allowed to
bring their families. Sometimes the parties were hard
to start. The guests did not know one another socially
but only as fellow-classmen. But the parties made a
great difference in their attitude toward one another
and toward the House. And they learned to use English in order to play with it, so to speak. I believe that
we never know a language until we have used it for
social, for non-useful, non-essential purposes. After
that we begin really to feel at home with it.

We have always emphasized dramatics. One of our
teachers insists that that is the best method of all for
teaching English to young people. Children will work
hard to change their habits of speaking in order to earn
the reward of having a part in a play. Something of

the same sort is seen in the work of the music school. Our teacher of music says that it is quite as easy to teach a child to enunciate clearly as to sing; the two things go together.

III

In the music school we have made an effort to have the children sing the songs that their parents brought with them from their own countries. The results have been very gratifying. The parents sing the songs at home until the children get them pretty well, and then they are practiced in the music room. Sometimes the parents themselves come to the music room to sing. We have always made a great point of having the children write out the music for these songs. It is as easy, we have found, for children who read music to write it as it is for them to read and write words. When the children have thoroughly learned the songs, they sing them back to their parents, and I assure you we have very enthusiastic audiences. . . .

IV

In all our work with the foreign born we have found that our own attitude toward them as aliens is most important. We may make their foreign birth a handicap to them and to us, or we may make it a very interesting and stimulating factor in their development and ours. You know that there is a theory of race which says that when people journeyed on foot or on camels or by other means into a strange part of the world, their contact with the established civilization there produced a curious excitement that often resulted in the creation of a new culture that never had existed before.

I believe that we may get, and should get, something of that sort of revivifying effect and upspringing of new culture from our contact with the groups who come to us from foreign countries, and that we can get it in no other way. This idea, I hope, we can always keep foremost in our minds in dealing with the foreign-born people in our midst.

We all know how the interdependence of men in modern life complicates the condition of their thinking, especially when they are facing a social situation in which certain values are but dimly emergent. Diverse social groups may fail altogether to tap the resources of such a situation, whereas a socially unified group might have found it comparatively easy. It is possible on the other hand for groups to find clues to a new life pattern in such situations of tension, for it is when old values are at hazard that new values get their first attention. The groups realize that the whole situation is calling for inner and outer adjustments, and the moment may give effective direction to half-formed purposes and may integrate them into usability. At times like these when diversified groups find all their old attitudes and assumptions transcended, they may receive together an impulsion toward new values. The foreign born through their very diversity have it in their power to unify American experience, if we accept John Dewey's statement that the general intelligence is dormant and its communications broken and faint until it possesses the public as its medium.

This, I think, is what the settlements are trying to do. They are trying to increase the public that shall be the medium for social developments that are of great moment to us all. They are trying to draw into participation in our culture large numbers of persons who would otherwise have to remain outside and who, being outside, would not only remain undeveloped themselves, but would largely cripple our national life and in the end would cripple our general development.

I am sure that anything we can do to widen the circle of enlightenment and self development is quite as rewarding to those who do it as to those for whom it is done.

14

Education
by the Current Event

Almost everything Addams wrote had to do with overcoming provincialism of one sort or another. Here she argues that discussion of local, national, and international occurrences can provide a means for overcoming the ignorance and prejudice that limit understanding between different groups of people — people of different ethnic and racial groups, of different nations, or simply of different persuasions.

The settlements early founded their educational theories upon a conviction that in every social grade and class in the whole circle of genuine occupations there are mature men and women of moral purpose and specialized knowledge, who because they have become efficient unto life, may contribute an enrichment to the pattern of human culture. We knew that much of this possible enrichment was lost because he who would incorporate these experiences into the common heritage must constantly depend upon fresh knowledge and must further be equipped with a wide and familiar acquaintance with the human spirit and its productions. The difficulties involved would be almost insurmountable but that life has a curious trick of suddenly regarding as a living moral issue, vital and

SOURCE: *The Second Twenty Years at Hull-House* (New York: Macmillan, 1930), chap. 12. Reprinted in shortened form in the *Survey* 64 (1930): 461–464.

unappeasable, some old outworn theme which has been kicked about for years as mere controversial material. The newly moralized issue, almost as if by accident, suddenly takes fire and sets whole communities in a blaze, lighting up human relationships and public duty with new meaning. The event suddenly transforms abstract social idealism into violent political demands, entangling itself with the widest human aspiration.

When that blaze actually starts, when the theme is heated, molten as it were with human passion and desire, the settlement can best use it in its unending effort to make culture and the issue of things go together. From time to time during the last twenty years, when such a blaze did start it seemed for the moment that the peculiar aspect of the world which marks each age for what it is—the summary of its experiences, knowledge and affections, in which are found the very roots of its social existence was fused into a glowing whole. At such a moment, it seemed possible to educate the entire community by a wonderful unification of effort and if the community had been able to command open discussion and a full expression of honest opinion the educational opportunity would have been incomparable.

II

As an example of sudden interest, resulting in widespread education upon a given theme, the trial at Dayton, Tennessee, upon the general subject of the theory of evolution, forms a striking example. . . .

During the trial the situation was so sharply defined that it brought before the entire country a public discussion of fundamentalism versus evolution. That such a situation arose was in one sense a demonstration of our democratic purpose, which is, after all, an attempt at self-expression for each man. Democracy believes that the man at the bottom may realize his aim only through an unfolding of his own being, and that he must have an efficacious share in the regulation of his own life. While there was no doubt that the over-whelming public opinion concerning the Tennessee trial was on the side of liberality both in politics and religion, the group of so-called narrow-minded men had made their own contribution to our national education. In the first place, they had asserted the actuality of religion. It is always difficult to convince youth that reality reaches upward as well as outward, and that the higher planes of life contain anything but chilly sentiments. The educator dealing with religious topics often finds that young people receive his statements with polite attention, but when it comes to action, they who are fretting with impatience to throw themselves into the stream of life and to become a part of its fast-flowing current, carefully imitate the really desirable world inhabited by successful men of affairs. But suddenly there came from a group of remote mountaineers a demonstration of a vivid and sustained interest in matters of religion, resulting in a sharp clash of doctrine between themselves and thousands of our fellow citizens, who all hung upon the issues of the trial with avid interest.

It was at times almost comic to hear the "hard-boiled" city youth in his bewilderment talk about the situation.

In the first place, modern economics had taught him —
or he thought that it had—that a man was abjectly
dependent upon the material world about him and
must succumb to the iron clamp which industry im-
poses upon life; moreover, the youth himself gravely
asserted that man's very freedom, morality and progress is determined by the material conditions which
surround him and he had bodily taken over this theory
into ethics and philosophy. He quoted those students
of the social order who in what they considered the
scientific spirit had collected and arranged data, to
demonstrate the sole reaction of economic forces upon
human life. These young people had for the most part
lightly disregarded all teleological considerations, as
they had long before renounced the theological explanations of a final cause. And yet many of them were
secretly glad of this opportunity for discussion with old
Jewish fathers who had never ceased to attest to the
life of the spirit and who on their side caught their first
glimpse in those sons hotly defending the theory of
evolution, of the same zeal which they and their fathers
had expended upon religion. These same young men
so devoted to economic determinism as a theory of life
had been already somewhat disconcerted by a recent
movement in psychiatry with the emphasis upon the
emotional and subconscious life versus the exclusive
response to environmental stimuli. But if they were
startled they were also much interested in this ardent
inner life which was apparently to be found among so
many different types of people who were everywhere
responding to the blaze of interest started in Tennessee.

The repercussions of the trial were the more interesting because the incident brought into the circle of

their discussion a large number of people who had hitherto been quite outside their zone of interest. These remote farmers were isolated, save on the occasional Sundays when a circuit rider came to preach, by their discouraging occupation of extracting a living from a rock-bound soil. Nothing could have been further from the experiences and mental processes of the intelligentsia of a cosmopolitan city than these mountaineers, nothing more diverse than the two methods of approach to the time-old question of the origin of man. Only a molten current event could have accomplished a simultaneous discussion upon the same theme by these two bodies of people.

Although these young Chicago intelligentsia I have been describing lived among colonies of immigrants, each one with its own history and conscious religious background, and had moreover naturally been interested in the normative sciences, they had known little about such descendants of early Americans so Anglo-Saxon and "Nordic" in background that they still had remnants of Elizabethan English in their daily speech. It was interesting to hear these young men talk of the effects of isolation whether the group were encompassed by mountains or by the invisible boundaries of a ghetto.

III

Another instance of discussion spreading to thousands of people in the United States was demonstrated when the Labor Party of England first came into power. While the discussion of such international events varies from community to community with local experiences, traditions and problems of human relationship, it has an enormous influence upon the situation as a whole. Many people for the first time get an impression of our own national situation in comparison with the economic situation in other nations and certain words lose their national connotation and more nearly approach international usage. The fact that in many European nations the socialists were among the major political parties, that a "Labor" Party had come to office in England was in itself an education in the use of words as they are current throughout civilization. Perhaps more important still the man of affairs began to contrast such attempts at political control of industrial situations with the associative business control which has been worked out in the United States. . . .

It would seem obvious that the most important condition for the peaceful and fruitful development of the world would be at the lowest, a theory of live and let live between countries organized on different economic systems. If the Soviet Republics are to foment revolution and unrest in countries where the basis of communism does not exist, and if countries organized by private business are determined to keep Russia outside the comity of nations, it is clear that the two economic systems will never learn much from one another. A mixed type of state with competitive and cooperative elements may have the greatest survival value and prove to be the most serviceable. But the line of demarkation between private business and public business will differ both between countries and in different stages in the same country. Obviously each country should have a basis of comparison and learn to work out its own opportunities both by the successes and failures of its world neighbors. Of course it ought to be possible to do this in the spirit of scientific detachment, for Russia is now conducting perhaps the largest piece of conscious social laboratory experiment that history records. It looks for the moment, however, as if Russia would evoke such a strong emotional reaction for so long a time that it will still remain impossible for Americans. . . .

IV

Another instance of education through the discussion of current social developments, took place in regard to the problem of race relations when the industrial needs of war-time and the immigration restriction following the war, resulted in a great increase of Negroes in the urban populations throughout the country. This was brought to a head in Chicago as in many other places by the question of housing, when real estate values became confused as always with the subject of segregation. Whatever may be the practical solution it is still true that a complete segregation of the Negro in definite parts of the city, tends in itself to put him outside the immediate action of that imperceptible but powerful social control which influences the rest of the population. Those inherited resources of civilization which are embodied in custom and kindly intercourse, make more for social restraint than does legal enactment itself. . . .

. . . Another result of race antagonism is the readiness to irritation which inevitably results when one race is forced to demand as a right from the other those things which should be accorded as a courtesy. Every chance meeting between representatives of the two races is easily characterized either by insolence or arrogance. To the friction of city life and the complications of modern intercourse is added this primitive race animosity.

Happily in the midst of this current event discussion, there came to Chicago a distinguished Negro singer, various plays concerning colored people which portrayed something of that inner life upon which the kinship of races is founded and the Race Relations Committee of the Chicago Woman's Club arranged for a week of exhibits at the Art Institute and for recitals and lectures by well-known artists, poets and scholars. We have no exact knowledge of what has been and is being lost by the denial of free expression on the part of the Negro, it is difficult even to estimate it. One can easily suggest the sense of humor, unique and spontaneous, so different from the wit of the Yankee or the inimitable story telling prized in the South; the natural use of rhythm and onomatopoeia which is now so often travestied in the grotesqueness of long words: the use of varied colors which makes it natural perhaps that the only scientific study made in America of the use of common clay as coloring material in the building of simple houses should have been done by a Negro so that we may hope some day to rival the pinks, yellows and blues of those European houses which afford the traveler such perpetual joy.

There is one exception to this lack of recognition, in the admiration of those melodies which we have learned to call the only American folksongs and which

have become the basis of the Negroes' contribution to
American music. Perhaps because an oppressed people have always been sustained by their dreams the
spirituals became the support of their failing spirits.
It may be that the wish-fulfillment was too slowly
transferred to actual life but certainly an ever-increas-
ing respect is coming from the Negroes' own achievements in the arts. Through their plays they have found
the stimulus for conduct in the very field where it was
possible to make the initial step toward social efficiency. It may be significant that the curtain falls on an
advanced play like "Porgy" while the Negroes of Cat-
fish Row are singing, "I'm on my way."

But even though fine demonstrations have been
made by smaller groups of cultivated Negroes, we cannot truthfully say, however much we should like to do
so, that recognition lies with the colored man himself
and that the worthy will be worthily received. To make
even the existing degree of recognition more general
requires first of all a modicum of leisure and freedom
from grinding poverty. An investigation made in 1929
by the Woman's Bureau of the Department of Labor
gives an analysis of *Colored Women in Industry* from
studies made in fifteen states. Their earnings were
found to be far below the earnings of most white women, although they too must somehow meet the expenses of food, shelter and clothing. A great American
industrialist had said, almost at the moment of the
publication of the report, "American industry must for
the future be based not on a living wage alone, nor
on a saving wage, but on a cultural wage." No one
needs the benefit of this dictum more than the ambitious Negro.

Because we are no longer stirred as the Abolitionists were, to remove fetters, to prevent cruelty, to lead the humblest to the banquet of civilization, we have allowed ourselves to become indifferent to the gravest situation in our American life. The abolitionists grappled with an evil intrenched since the beginning of recorded history and it seems at moments that we are not even preserving what was so hardly won. To continually suspect, suppress or fear any large group in a community must finally result in a loss of enthusiasm for that type of government which gives free play to the self-development of a majority of its citizens. It means an enormous loss of capacity to the nation when great ranges of human life are hedged about with antagonism. We forget that whatever is spontaneous in a people, in an individual, a class or a nation, is always a source of life.

In the world-wide effort to relieve the colored races from the odium and discrimination which white races have placed upon them, no man living on the planet today has done more than has Mahatma Gandhi, first in South Africa in the struggle for civil rights against the Transvaal Government, which absorbed his energy for almost twenty years, and later in the undertaking, the most difficult of all, directed against customs intrenched in the religious traditions of India, to free the fifty million untouchables or pariahs, who are subject to many harsh rules of segregation. While the differences of race between the Brahmans and Pariahs is not the sole basis of the insupportable division between them, the situation is essentially the same as that which faces any effort to break down barriers of race or caste. Gandhi's most striking success in his protest against untouchability was the opening of the roads, which because they passed near the temples were forbidden to the Pariahs. His followers faced a cordon of police for twelve hours every day during a year and four months before the orthodox Brahmans yielded. Such devotion opened to the untouchables not only that one forbidden road but all the roads that had been forbidden to them in southern India and gave the doctrine of untouchability its severest blow. Such a long and courageous effort may indicate that only sustained moral energy will be able to break through long established restrictions. . . .

. . . Problems of race relations may arise in situations where a group of people regard themselves, or are regarded by others, as racially homogeneous, even where such an assumption does not correspond to scientific reality. Merely to inform people that such and such a group conflict is based upon an ethnological misunderstanding, will not do away either with the conflict or its emotional associations in the minds of those implicated. The entire race situation demonstrates once more that mere information is not enough and that the various research bodies need to be constantly supplemented. . . .

[Section V has been omitted.]

VI

During its first two decades, Hull-House with other American settlements, issued various studies and fact-finding analyses of the city areas with which they were most familiar. The settlements had antedated by three years the first sociological departments in the universities and by ten years the establishment of the first Foundations so that in a sense we were the actual pioneers in field research. We based the value of our efforts not upon any special training, but upon the old belief that he who lives near the life of the poor, he who knows the devastating effects of disease and vice, has at least an unrivaled opportunity to make a genuine contribution to their understanding. . . .

. . . In the third decade of our existence [we developed] as a sort of settlement creed [the conviction] that the processes of social amelioration are of necessity the results of gradual modification. We learned to act upon a belief that the hoary abominations of society can only be done away with through the "steady effort to accumulate facts and exalt the human will." But because such an undertaking requires the coöperation of many people and because with the best will in the world it is impossible to get the interest of the entire community centered upon any given theme, we gradually discovered that the use of the current event is valuable beyond all other methods of education. In time we came to define a settlement as an institution attempting to learn from life itself in which undertaking we did not hesitate to admit that we encountered many difficulties and failures. . . .

The settlements have often been accused of scattering their forces; as institutions they are both philanthropic and educational; in their approach to social problems they call now upon the sociologist, now upon the psychiatrist; they seek the services of artists, economists, gymnasts, case-workers, dramatists, trained nurses; one day they beg the anthropologist for a clue to a new immigration, and the next they boast that one of their pupils is playing in the symphony orchestra. In response to the irrefutable charge of weakness in multiform activity, we are accustomed to reply that even so we are not as varied and complex as life itself. I recall my sense of relief the first time I heard a sociologist use the phrase, "vortex causation"; the universities were at last defining the situation and it was possible that they would later enter this innerrelated field of personal difficulties, bewildering legal requirements, ill health and conflicting cultures which the settlements find so baffling. . . .

. . . Each current event in this interrelated world may be the result of a repercussion from any part of the globe, or due to the same impulse manifesting itself in widely separated areas. . . .

. . .It seems at moments as if we were about to extend indefinitely what we call our public, and that unless it were stretched to world dimensions, the most significant messages of our times might easily escape us.

Acknowledgments

Grateful acknowledgment is made for permission to reprint articles or chapters from books by Jane Addams in this anthology:

Selection 8 (The House of Dreams): Reprinted with permission of John A. Brittain from *The Spirit of Youth and the City Streets*. Copyright 1909 by Macmillan Publishing Company.

Selection 11 (Recreation as a Public Function in Urban Communities): Reprinted with permission of The University of Chicago Press from the *American Journal of Sociology* 17 (1912): 615–619. © 1912 by The University of Chicago. All rights reserved.

Selection 12 (Moral Education and Legal Protection for Children): Reprinted with permission of Macmillan Publishing Company from *A New Conscience and an Ancient Evil* by Jane Addams. Copyright 1912 by Macmillan Publishing Company.

Selection 13 (Widening the Circle of Enlightenment: Hull House and Adult Education): Reprinted with permission of the American Association for Adult and Continuing Education from the *Journal of Adult Education* 2 (1930): 276–279.

Selection 14 (Education by the Current Event): Reprinted with permission of Macmillan Publishing Company from *The Second Twenty Years at Hull-House*